URBAN MYTHS

Phil Healey
and
Rick Glanvill

Virgin

Dedicated to Frances, Yael and Ollie, and our families and friends (of friends).

828. 91407

First published in Great Britain in 1992 by
Virgin Books
an imprint of Virgin Publishing Ltd
338 Ladbroke Grove
London W10 5AH

ISBN 0 86369 686 4

Cover illustration by Richard Adams

Typeset by Type Out, London, SW16.

Printed and bound in Great Britain by
Cox & Wyman Ltd, Reading, Berkshire

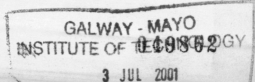

ACKNOWLEDGEMENTS

Phil Healey and Rick Glanvill would like to thank the following people and places for sharing their mythical knowledge with them:

Tony Ageh, Robin Allen, Mick Armson, Sarah Ball, Albert Becker, Penny 'Ounces to the pound' Brunton, Andy Brice, Bill Broadhead, Billy Budd, Martin 'Woosie' Bullock, Roy Carr, Gez 'Spexo' Casey, Clare the printer, Yael, Yona and Miriam Cohen, Paul 'Big Ears', 'Blabbermouth', 'Juggler', 'Crojo' Crome, Diane Taylor, Julie Douglas, Big John Eichler, Andy Forbes-Gower, Bobbie, Johnny, Gary and Sarah Glanvill (the Glanvills), Steve Glennon, Bobby Greenland, Richard Greenleaf, Peter Hanington, Dave Heywood, Irene, Ray and Nigel Healey (the Healeys), David Hurran, Ian Hutchings, Joe at the *Guardian,* Joe from Lagos, Scott and Mary Johnston (the Johnstons), Stuart Jones, Jamie Keenan, Dave Kimberley, Frances Lloyd, Guy Lloyd, John 'Squaddie' Ludlam, Michael Patrick Aloysius McCoy, Dave Martin, Chris Morris, Al Nicholls, Chris Padmore, Al and Ceri Preston (the Prestons), Dave 'the Avenger' and Jessica Rigg, Kathy Rooney, 'Barney' McCarthy, Steve Rumney, John Sandford, Satwinder 'Turban Myths' Sehmi, John 'Skins' Skinner, Willie Smax, Sue Smallwood, Peter 'Spanking' Spanton, Hilary Steele, Wg Cmdr Alex Stewart, Mick Suett, Dave Talbot, Chris Tarrant, Mark 'Urgent' Urgent, Martin Vallis, Nigel Vernon, Carol Wilhide, Chippy Wood, Tim Woolgar; the Three Kings of Clerkenwell, Vic Naylor's and The Hope, Smithfield.

CONTENTS

Introduction
x

Urban Classics
Popular stories that everyone tells
1

Technophobia
The treachery of mean machines
19

Car Trouble
Horsepower horseplay
40

The rocking Robin; Spark out; Up north; Auf wiedersehen Trabbie; The driving dog; Inertia reel sick-belt; Dad's pull-over; Mythellaneous

The Long Arm of the Law
Arresting tales of brushes with authority
49

Double-take; Fat filly foils felony; The one-legged bandit; Rag week roadworks; Blue light spells danger; Number plate giveaway; Backwards in the fast lane; 'This is a pick-up!'; Get the picture; Mythellaneous

Demon Drink
Tales of the tipple that topples
60

The office party and Mr Byrite; Dead man's handle; The man from Dudley; The sickly city slicker; Terminally drunk; Keep it up your sleeve; The night stalker; A stable environment; Shire indulgence; Yer 'tis; Mythellaneous

Food for Thought
Awful à la carte anecdotes
69

Dog's dinner; Chinese poodle; Southern-fried rodent; Pie-eyed; Handy loaf; Nowt taken out; An offal experience; Sick as a . . .; Bistro bog bother; Russian bangers; Keep it under your hat; Pea brain; Peanut; Fruity salad; The runner, Mythellaneous

Man's Best Friends
The animal kingdom at its least predictable

The dead rabbit; The hungry Chihuahuas; Sex with Nanny; Roach-prints; The snappy crocodile; The Labrador let-off; The scorpion 'down under'; Parrot fashion; Paws for thought; Monkey-hanging business; Billy the Seal; The purring engine; 'Hangdog' Hannah; Grandma's toes; Uncool for cats; 'Green Goddess' cat; The S-bend snake; The cannibal wolfhound; Trunk and disorderly; Not too trilled; Yucky Yucca; Coming a cropper; Home sweet homer; Anticlimax; Bacon lined; Dirty dog; Posing pouch; Having a truffle; The dead budgie; Mythellaneous

Occupational Hazards
Weird tales from the workplace

The deer-stalker; Blackout; Lift logger; Papier man-mâché; Green side up; 'Who's a naughty boy, then?'; Baptism of fire; The unlucky ladders; The carpet creeper; The hand bag; Tube runner; Plumbing new depths; Log roll; Incoming tax; Mythellaneous

Military Myths
Over the top escapades

Header; Down and out; The amputee-escapee; Shot in the dark; Spud-U-lob; Crater disturbance; War game pie; Heat-seeking rissole; Flipperin' dangerous; Mythellaneous

Travel Sickness
The perils lurking in foreign parts
133

The ring of confidence; The burning deck; Odd customs; Out of the fishing boat, into the fire; Sun basting; Legless in Gaza; The flame-haired toupée of Thika; 'Be'ind you!'; Handy for the beach; Swiss rolled; Board and logic; The naked ski-girl; Private viewing; Rollerballs; Long-haul lamb; Welcome to Dallas; Mythellaneous

New York Stories
Maggoty myths from the Big Apple
150

Bombed out at JFK; The kidney burglar; The Empire State escape; 'Hit the deck, lady'; The buggering Bronx Batman

Under the Knife
Mythical medical mayhem
156

Gone to seed; The farm hand; Re-animation; Aorta know better; She never even knew she was pregnant; Flushed with embarrassment; Four eyes only; Scal-pal; The hair nest; The back eye; False leg fight; The tooth fairy; Medium-wave molars; Sticky situation; Wagging it; Given the slip; Eye eye; Cavity wall filling; Mythellaneous

X-rated
On-the-job jams
169

Kinky K.O.; Lovers' lock; No small parts; A sad reflection; Chicken gobble; Give and give; Fit for nothing; Tits first;

The arty man's peculiar habit; Third leg thrombosis; These boots were made for wanking; The photocopier philanderers; Revenge is . . .; Pipe down, sir; The botty bottle; Rampant but broken; Suds law; Bangkok Bill; Doggie-collar fashion; More cake, vicar?; Sofa, so bad; Below the belt; Mythellaneous

Wedded Bliss
Nuptial nonsense
The plastered groom; Mr and Mrs; Hostile reception; Ultra-violet embarrassment; Up and under; Blue wedding video; Mythellaneous

Friends and Relations
With friends like these, who needs relatives?
Atlantic potion; A fart amongst friends; That sinking feeling; Going down; The yuppies' saucy neighbours; The Xmas family break-in; The spurned wife; Down the hatch; The old man and the teeth; The hyperactive zoo child; The coveted pom-pom hat; Par for pa; This little piggy extra; Sunday best, personal best; Go ferret; Brick house; Ewe must be joking; Fall Guy; Mythellaneous

Wanted

Bibliography

INTRODUCTION

This book is a collection of urban myths, legends and apocryphal tales. You will probably have heard something like these entertaining fables whether you realise it or not. The stories are saucy, implausible, bizarre and scary, yet strangely moral, and usually told by someone who claims they know the main protagonists — or at least friends of theirs do. Once that link has been established, for some reason we all want to believe them, no matter how far-fetched and ridiculous the plot.

As with all the best yarns, there's a spooky ring of truth about them. It could easily be you dropping a brimming chamber pot through a conservatory roof (*The chamber pot*), being blown up on the lavatory (*Hot hog*), or finding a tomato plant growing up into your brain (*Gone to seed*). And that's just a sample of the odd twists of fate recounted in these comical cautionary tales, embellished and adapted through countless retellings, and now captured here in the biggest collection of urban myths ever put together.

In a society obsessed by gossip, urban myths are the best unfounded stories around. You can hear them told anywhere there's an audience — from the smoky pub to the swanky dinner party.

However, when it comes to defining what an urban myth is, it's maybe easier to say what they are not. As the name suggests, these are not rural folk tales. Their neuroses are those of the industrial concrete jungle rather the country village. Mother Nature, when she does appear in urban myths, is regarded with deep suspicion or contempt by city-dwellers — and with just cause, as *The dead rabbit* and *The night stalker* amply prove.

These myths are not jokes, though some of them have wicked punchlines; they are not horror stories, although many of them are decidedly disturbing; and they are not true stories, though they may have evolved from some half-forgotten real event. They span all these categories and more, and are part of a thriving oral tradition that strikes a chord in every one of us.

Urban myths mostly share a common formula. Nearly all are testaments to people's vanity, stupidity or resourcefulness, and shaky grasp of reality. They nag away at our paranoias and irrational fears, especially concerning life's rituals like getting married, getting drunk, working, courting, going to parties, eating out, or driving, dying, DIY-ing, and, most perilous of all, going to the toilet.

They can be finely honed anecdotes, shaggy dog stories or vague tales about wild cats on suburban heaths, but always with an outlandish turn of events that distorts the comfortable picture. The more these stories are retold, customised and passed on, the more poignant they become. That's the beauty of urban myths: they are universal and local; ageless and constantly updated to retain their freshness. It's a testament to the strength of urban myths that many have endured for generations, and they cut across barriers of age, class, race and gender.

All this has made urban myths the stock-in-trade of the tabloid newspapers. During summer's 'silly season', stories very much like *The farm hand, The driving dog* and *Yucky Yucca* regularly appear as unattributed 'fillers'.

This is part of the life cycle of some urban myths. A half-remembered story appears in the paper or on the radio and, with the twist that a Chinese Whisper always gives, does the conversational rounds before appearing in the press again the following season, radically re-modelled.

But there's an undercurrent, too. The world of myths is one of deep-seated fears and prejudices, moral and social warnings. They preach moderation in all things (*Blue light spells danger*); trust the experts (*Overhaul*); stick to your own class (*That sinking feeling*); new technology can be a snake or a ladder (*Auto-pirate*); be smart, but not too smart (*Cashpoint Charlie*); and if you must break the law, be lucky (*Backwards in the fast lane*). It's a world where you can't trust anything or anyone — least of all yourself.

Urban myths are bonding tales. They kick-start a conversation, bolster the bar-room bore and, unlike jokes, require little skill in the way you tell 'em: the plot is generally funny enough without a song and dance.

This book serves another purpose as well. Urban myths are a safety valve for our illogical phobias. We all love a cataclysmic cock-up, and we can laugh at any predicament when there is someone so patently, haplessly worse off than ourselves, like most of the unfortunates featured here.

Healey and Glanvill's *Urban Myths* is not a sociological study, more a celebration of the ingenuity and vitality of a living verbal tradition. We sacrificed hours to a painstaking gathering of these sparkling conversation pieces, sometimes forced against our will to spend evening after evening in seedy drinking establishments and ribald company. We only hope you have as much fun reading and passing them on as we did researching them.

URBAN CLASSICS

Popular stories that everyone tells

The following are the universal myths you hear told and retold up and down the country, enduring old favourites among everyone from playground children to supping pensioners. For some odd reason, the violently demented seem over-represented in this area — possibly the horror aspect makes them all the more memorable or harder to forget. These archetypal apocryphal tales are time-honoured standards of the quintessential urban myth. They span the spectrum of colourful yarns, from toe-curling cases of social disgrace, to unsavoury episodes involving dumb animals.

The hairy hand

Late one night, my uncle's old school mate was driving home from Whitechapel to Barking. At the time, there had been a number of savage attacks on women waiting for late-night buses, and this was, of course the old stalking ground of Jack The Ripper. It was dark, foul weather — windy, and really bucketing it down — and as he was driving through Stepney, he saw a woman crouched under a bus stop. With the thought of this attacker around, he decided to stop and give her a lift at least some part of her journey. So he pulled up and the drenched figure got in. He began trying to make conversation with his passenger, who he noted was well-built and didn't know how to apply make-up properly, but to no avail.

Several attempts having led to nothing but a grunt, the driver took a sneaky closer look, and noticed to his consternation that the hands clutched round the handbag were extremely hairy and muscular. The more he looked at the person next to him, the more he panicked.

He decided on a plan. 'Could you just nip out quickly and check my back lights?' he asked, 'because that car just flashed me and I think they might not be working.' The shady figure obliged. The driver slammed the door shut, rammed the accelerator to the floor and sped to the nearest police station. As he screeched to a halt outside, he noticed that the 'woman' had left the handbag in the front, so he presented it for inspection when he nervously burbled his story.

'Looks like you've had a lucky escape, sir,' said the duty sergeant, producing from the bag a shiny, blood-stained hatchet.

One of the authors' uncles related this yarn over ten years ago, and still maintains it happened exactly like that. When it was pointed out that similar stories of hirsute, axe-wielding t.v.s have circulated all over UK cities for years (notably Chapeltown in Leeds during the time of the Yorkshire Ripper), he gave us an old-fashioned look.

The fingered felon

This Glasgow couple I heard about went out for the evening. When they got back in the house later, they were greeted by their pit-bull terrier, but he seemed more subdued than usual. Then he started choking and wretching, so they patted him increasingly hard on the back, but to no avail. They looked up an emergency vet and rushed him round there.

The vet opened the pit-bull's mouth and looked in, then said he could see something blocking its throat. Because the dog was so vicious, he put him under sedation before removing the obstruction. It turned out to be two bloody human fingers.

'I should ring the police,' said the vet, handing them the phone.

The couple rushed home to meet the police, who set about searching the house. In an upstairs bedroom, there was a trail of blood leading to a wardrobe. Inside cowered a would-be burglar clutching his mutilated hand, and unconscious from loss of blood.

The poodle in the microwave

A rich elderly lady from Harrogate was taking her pet poodle out for a walk when they were caught in a downpour. Rushing back inside, fretful for her pampered pet, she was desperate to dry him out and warm him up as soon as possible. So she took him straight into the kitchen, opened the door of her daughter's new microwave cooker for the first time, and thrust him in, moving the dial to a moderate setting. She patted his head and carefully closed the door with a click.

The old lady was still drying her hair when the cooked dog exploded, ripping the door off the microwave.

> A popular 'tabloids' story, this one. Some people tell the 12″ extended play version which suggests that the woman placed the hapless dog in the microwave because she'd become used to putting it in her old electric cooker for a minute or two to warm up when this sort of drenching had occurred in the past — an echo of the other story about the babysitters putting the little one's head in the gas oven for a minute to slip it back into the land of nod. It's also sometimes mischievously added that the woman sued the manufacturer of the hi-tech appliance over the incident . . . and won her case, because it didn't say anywhere in the instructions that you shouldn't dry off your poodle inside the contraption. [See also **Technophobia**]

The vanishing hitchhiker

A friend of a friend was cruising down the A1 to London, when he passed a young lady standing by the side of the road. He pulled up and asked her if she needed a lift. Without speaking, she got into the car. He was quite attracted to her, so he tried to get her talking, but she just wouldn't say anything, not even where she was getting off. Instead, at the junction, she pointed. Then at her road, and then at her house, where she got out of the car. He drove off in a huff.

A couple of days later, he was looking for something in the car when he came across a woman's coat. Knowing it must the hitchiker's, he retraced his route to return the coat to her. So he knocked on the door and an older lady opened it. He held out the coat and explained that he wanted to return it to the young woman. The woman burst into tears 'Yes, it was my daughter's', she spluttered, 'but she was killed on the A1 five years ago.'

The Edinburgh skinheads

A TV producer's brother-in-law took his wife and kids to Edinburgh for the weekend in their posh station wagon. One day during their stay, they parked in the city centre and went on a sightseeing tour. They were a bit concerned when they returned to the car to see that it was surrounded and sat-upon by about a dozen aggressive-looking skinheads. You could say he was over-reacting, but the brother-in-law got upset and lost his temper when they were slow in getting off his nice car. The situation got a bit hairy between them, so the wife and kids jumped inside and locked the doors. A proper altercation seemed to be avoided when the bloke quickly jumped into his car, slammed the door and drove away — slowly, at first, to make out he wasn't afraid.

But it didn't end there. His kids pointed out that one of the skinheads was running behind, and shouting obscenities at them. The bloke put his foot down a bit, but the skinhead was still running and shouting his head off, and his mates were coming as well now. So the bloke really gave it the gun, and the car was going about 50 mph. The skinhead sounded demented now, but was still behind them, though god knows how, thought the bloke. Finally, the skinhead fell down in the road, and they steamed off. A few miles on, the bloke pulled over, sweating, and got out to see if the skinheads had damaged the car at all. To his surprise he found no harm, but three ringed and severed fingers caught in the bumper, with tattooed letters spelling 'L' 'O' and 'V' . . .

> A new twist on an old story of social mistrust.
> For skinheads, you might read Rastas, Hell's
> Angels, or even grizzly bears [see also Paws
> for thought, **Man's Best Friends**].

Upstairs, downstairs

There was a babysitter working for a well-off family I knew in Sheffield who one evening received some disturbing phone calls. At first they were just heavy breathing, but when the caller began to threaten murder and made it clear he knew where she was, the babysitter rang the police. It was a huge house and quite spooky anyway.

The police were very good, and told her they'd immediately put a trace on the calls, and to keep the bloke talking next time. A little later, the phone rang again. It was the same caller, so she strung him along as much as she could, even though he was saying the most blood-curdling and offensive things to her. Eventually he hung up. But the phone rang again straight away. It was the police.

'Get out of there immediately!' shouted an officer. 'We traced the call, and it was the other phone line at your house. The nutter's upstairs!'

> Variations on this theme have been the stuff of
> shoestring budget horror movies for decades.
> Sometimes, as in the Audrey Hepburn movie
> *After Dark*, the threatened woman is blind, or
> the caller is the policeman himself.

The hook

Many years back, a young couple were canoodling in a lovers' lane on the edge of town. The radio was playing and the car was well steamed up. The lovers' clinch was broken when a stern voice interrupted the light programme and announced that a local criminal asylum had reported a breakout and that there was a homicidal maniac on the prowl. The man was extremely dangerous and should on no account be approached. He was easily identifiable, it said, as he had a very distinguishing feature — a hook instead of a hand on one arm.

The announcement sent a shiver down the girl's spine and

thoroughly put the dampers on her ardour. She insisted on being driven home immediately. Chronically dischuffed, the boyfriend started the car and sped off back to her parents' at a rate of knots. When they got back, the boyfriend, ever the gent, went round to open her door, and was horrified to find a steely hook dangling from the handle.

The maniac on the roof

A lass someone at college knew was travelling in her boy-friend's car late at night through the New Forest, when their car suddenly started spluttering and stalled. They'd run out of petrol in the middle of nowhere. At first she thought it might be a ruse by her bloke to get a bit of rural slap and tickle, but the concern on his face soon scotched that. It was pitch black, and the only light they could see was coming from what looked like a mansion or hospital some miles away. The boyfriend told her to lock the doors and wait while he went for help.

Hours passed, and still no sign of him. She was beginning to get very nervous. Still more time went by, when she was startled by a horrendous banging on the back, then top of the car. Before she could scream, the car was surrounded by police cars with lights flashing and sirens wailing.

A voice over a loud-hailer told her: 'Get out of the car slowly, walk steadily towards the police line, and don't, repeat don't, look around.' She did as she was told, but as she neared the police line, she couldn't stop herself looking round at the car to see what was making the awful thumping noise . . . only to see an escaped psychopath banging her boyfriend's severed head on the car roof.

> Real playgound specials, these ones, with versions for ever region. Often the couple are newly-weds, and sometimes the setting is in France, seemingly littered with expatriate corpses. Read on . . .

Roll out the dead carpet

There was a family from Surrey who decided to spend their vacation in France, taking their elderly grandma with them. Granny spent all their stay complaining. Well, not quite all of it, because a little way into the holiday, she died on them.

Deciding that the old woman would hate not to be buried in her beloved Blighty, the family set about returning her home, and, mindful of the customs and other problems they might face, they resolved to hide her. So they bought a cheap bit of carpet, and rolled the wrinkled little corpse up in it. Granny's body was by now too stiff to bend on to a car seat, so they had to strap her on the roof-rack. In this way she was driven across France for two days, through driving rain and baking sunshine, across the Channel by ferry, and finally all the way home.

Unhappily, having made it back without a hitch, the family were devastated when, after a well-earned cuppa, they went outside to find the car had been stolen — carpet, Granny and all. And they were never recovered.

We've heard of numerous international
versions of this classic dilemma. In the States,
the trip is to Mexico, and in Spain, it's to
Portugal . . .

Travel bug

A woman well-known to our family friends was the travelling
type, always hopping off to exotic places. One year, she set
her heart on Guatemala in Central America. She went with
an adventure holiday tour, which took people into the wild
interior — lots of hacking through jungle with a machete and
bivouacking overnight amidst the sounds of the rainforest.
The woman was game and loved roughing it, so she wasn't
at all fazed by all the creepie-crawlies everywhere, and had
one of the best holidays she could remember.

When she returned home to England, she noticed that a
bite on her cheek she had sustained early on in the jungle
had not healed up and was beginning to itch. She put some
cream on it and thought no more about.

After a few days, however, the swelling had grown very
bad indeed, and soon, despite applying various creams, the
woman looked in the mirror and saw the whole cheek was
red, itchy and inflamed. Finally, finding the irritation too
much, the woman gave her cheek a really good scratch. At
which the skin cracked, and hundreds of tiny spiders burst
out, scattering away across her face.

Which all goes to show: never trust Incy-
Wincy, the unpredictable little arachnid with

anti-personnel habits. Paradoxically, in classic African myth, 'Anansi the spider' is a resourceful hero to be admired and emulated.

[*See also* Yucky Yucca, **Man's Best Friends**]

The goat

Some friends were on an angling holiday in north Cornwall, sea-fishing off the cliffs. The fish were refusing to bite, and not much was happening generally, until one of the blokes went wandering and discovered an abandoned stone well half-buried among some bushes.

They decided to see how deep it was by dropping a small pebble into the shaft. The stone whistled down the echoey chasm and eventually splashed quietly at the bottom. So they threw a bigger rock down, then an even bigger one. It was much more fun than fishing.

Eventually one of the blokes found a large steel spike and threw that down. As he did, there was a sudden rustling in the shrubbery.

The lads noticed the bar was attached to a long chain, which began to rattle through the grass, gathering momentum, until suddenly a tethered goat burst through the bushes, was dragged past them bleating frantically, and hurtled down the well.

Other settings for this billy goat gaffe you may have come across include ski resorts near deep crevasses, the Lake District with its deep pot-holes, and rocky parts of Spain.

The man in the back

A Cardiff woman was driving home alone one dark night, and came up to a slip road on to the M5. There wasn't that much traffic, so she was putting her foot down a bit. But as she got on to the motorway, she looked ahead of her and was alarmed to see what looked like a little child lying down by the hard shoulder. She screeched to a halt and immediately ran to see if she could help.

When she got closer, though, she saw that it was just a big, lifelike doll. She was relieved and returned to her car, but as she did, a dark car, going quite slowly, cruised up behind hers, flashing its headlamps at her. Not a little concerned that this might turn nasty, she decided to hurry home a.s.a.p.

But as she roared off, the car stuck close to her, following her every detour and flashing again and again. She then realised this was a pretty threatening situation, and as there was no-one at her home, headed instead for her friend's house. The car was now trying to overtake her, and there was a shadowy figure in the driving seat waving his hands around aggressively.

Finally, she swerved to a halt by her friend's house and ran out. The bloke in the other car dashed out, ran up to her and said 'Wait! I was trying to warn you! When you stopped before, someone got in the back of your car.' They both looked round, to see a thin, raggedy man scampering away down the road.

> This is a typical urban myth about the danger
> of making snap assumptions, and how the threat
> can come from unforeseen areas.

The chamber pot

A mate from college got friendly with a rich kid and was invited to a party at the latter's 'country retreat'. He accepted and was looking forward to a glimpse of how the other half lives.

The house was amazing – a real mansion – absolutely massive and in enormous grounds. My mate felt well out of his depth, but really enjoyed himself and got so drunk he virtually had to be carried to his room on the second floor.

He woke up in the middle of the night needing to relieve himself, and with a wicked headache. He knew there was a chamber pot under the bed, because he'd had a good laugh at it when he arrived, but he wanted to do number twos and it would've been embarrassing to do it in a pot. So he left his room and set off to find the toilet in the house's labyrinths. He looked all along the corridor, but every door had a snoring occupant behind it, so he gave up and resolved to use the chamber pot after all. Much relieved, he drifted back to sleep.

In the morning he was woken by a bell and cries to come down for breakfast, but he needed to have a leak first, which he did, and then decided that, sober, he'd easily find a toilet where he could flush away the pot's contents.

Leaving the offending porcelain behind, he looked along the corridor and again couldn't locate the WC. Giving up on it, and still a little tipsy, he thought he might as well throw the stuff out of his window on to the grounds where no one would notice. So he slid up the sash window, lifted up the brimming chamber pot and leaned out to see where he could pour.

Unfortunately, the handle broke, and the pot fell down the

side of the house, crashing through the glass conservatory roof below, smashing, and splashing its contents all over the main table where the other guests were enjoying their continental breakfast.

Without a word, the poor lad rushed into his clothes, out the front door, and hurtled along the drive in his car.

> But it doesn't end there. This is the follow-up
> story some people tell . . .

Some time later, he concluded that his behaviour — even drunk — had been appalling, and decided to go back during the week to apologise to the lady of the house, which he did.

When he rang the sash bell, the butler came to the door, and explained that her ladyship was in a meeting at the moment, but would the young man care to wait for her in the library?

He sauntered nervously into the dull room, picked up a dusty book and sat down on the sofa. As he sat, he heard a yelp. He got up straight away and looked down to see what he'd sat on. Regrettably, it was the lady's Chihuahua, and it was now very dead.

The secretary's sexy surprise

A middle-aged boss was feeling the years slipping away from him and sensed his frisky days might be numbered, and was trying his best to forget it was his birthday again — the big 5-0. His family seemed to be doing likewise. There was no mention of his special day at breakfast, and his wife even said that she was going to the theatre that night. He imagined he might spend his birthday alone in front of the telly. So when his charming young secretary suggested they might go out for a drink after work, he jumped at the idea (and hoped for another jump later). The two had a nice evening, and with each cocktail he was getting hotter for her. Eventually she suggested she drive him back to his place. When they arrived there, he put his arm around her and implored her to come in for a coffee – it was still quite early.

Once inside, the secretary ran ahead of him, turned out the lights and led him into the living-room and told him to stay there while she 'fixed up a special birthday treat for him'. Imagining that the nature of this treat was sexual, the boss began hurriedly to remove all his clothes.

Minutes later, as he stood in naked, fumbling anticipation of what was about to happen, all the lights suddenly went on, and he was confronted by all his family, friends and workmates shouting 'Surprise!!'

> Another version of this well-worn tale involves a couple coming back from a romantic meal for two celebrating their wedding anniversary, who feel a bit fruity, go into the front room and strip off. They are caught naked, *in flagrante delicto*, when their friends burst in with the traditional 'Surprise!!'

Vatman

A gang of workmen were renovating a big old house. The

previous owner, a very rich, very old woman, had lived most of her life in the old colonial West Indies.

The new owners wanted everything done to the place, and it was a long job that occupied the workers all throughout the long hot summer months.

Their labours were made more pleasant by the discovery in the early weeks of a huge wooden cask in the dusty basement, which they soon found to be full of rum. The labourers knew of the house's Caribbean connection, and bored a hole in the side of the vat, partaking liberally of what they guessed to be the finest Jamaican rum. Just the thing after a hot day's grafting.

Towards the end of the summer, as they were putting the finishing touches to the house, they polished off the last of the rum, and, as the basement was the last area to be worked on, decided to break up the cask that had given them so much pleasure.

As they attacked the old vat with hammers, however, they got a bit of a nasty shock. Inside, they found the perfectly preserved cadaver of the old woman's husband, shipped back from Jamaica in the only thing that was guaranteed to keep him properly embalmed for the journey home.

A strong variation told to us more recently goes as follows:

As everybody knows dockers are always helping themselves to whatever cargo happens to be around. One day a large container was delivered to Liverpool docks. The foreman warned his subordinates to leave it well alone. And if they did, he'd turn a blind eye to all the other pilfering.

But the temptation was too great, especially after they worked out the container was full of liquid. The dockers quickly put a tap on it, someone took a swig and discovered it was alcohol. They were all soon four sheets to the wind.

The foreman came back and, shaking his head, got the drunken dockers to open the top. Inside the container was a huge pile of severed arms and legs. They'd been preserved in alcohol for medical purposes.

MYTHELLANEOUS

The Wild Animals of Britain

★ The Surrey Puma

★ The big black cats of the Peak District that sneak through cat-flaps and bite housewives' bottoms

★ The teeming wallabies, also of the Peak District

★ The black cat of Haldon Moor, south Devon, that worries sheep (and puts the wind up the locals)

★ The escaped pet crocodiles that thrive near the power station outlets on the River Trent

★ Rosie the 30-stone pig in the New Forest, scourge of the picnickers

★ Nessie, the Loch Ness Monster – and family

★ Hercules the twelve-foot tall, Equity card-holding Grizzly, loose in the Highlands after shooting a TV commercial

★ Coypus, imported for their fur, running amok in East Anglia

★ Scorpions at Ongar station

★ Two-headed sheep at Windscale

★ Parrots in Cornwall

★ The super-rat of London's sewers

★ The Mersey Salmon

TECHNOPHOBIA

The treachery of mean machines

The old-fogey's fear of the new-fangled, where every inno-
vation begets a spanner-in-the works apprehension. The
myths contained in this section are probably the most
ludicrously implausible of the whole lot, partly because
they're conjured up by people who think machines are out
to get us. When you're a small cog in the big wheel of
fortune, the micro-chips-with-everything mentality is sure
to dish out nervous breakdowns. One thing's for sure. These
vicious devices may save labour, but they definitely won't
save face. . . .

Hot hog

A bloke my uncle knows who was mad about motorbikes recently came into some money, and decided to spend it on one of those brand new Harley Davidsons.

The bike was his pride and joy, he was always buffing it and polishing it. He even put carpet on the floor of his garage. Forever boasting about just how great his bike was, he was always on about doing a ton, MPG, cruising speed, acceleration and the like — ride to live, live to ride, etc.

One day he was having a party round his house and his friends bet him he couldn't ride his huge bike up the stairs. After a few shandies, the bloke, eager to prove them wrong, revved up his 'hog' and hurtled up the stairs. But he lost momentum halfway up and the heavy bike tumbled sideways crushing the rider's leg. He was hauled off to hospital leaving the bike lying on its side in the kitchen.

The bloke's wife came home from the hospital and started to clear up. She mopped up the spilt petrol and, for want of somewhere better to put it, tipped the fuel down the outside lav.

A few hours later the bloke came back in the ambulance with his leg in plaster to the hip, feeling pretty dischuffed. After a cup of tea he was busting to go to the loo. But because of his leg cladding, he couldn't get up the stairs so he went outside, plonked himself down and lit a consolation fag, and the bog exploded.

That one's been reproduced in the *Guardian*,
so it must be true.

Blind-spot welding

A mate who's crazy about cars told me of an old auto enthusiast he'd heard about who had been spot welding on his old banger. He had all the gear: protective gloves, overalls and dark welding goggles — the lot.

But one particular day he was welding away and lifted his goggles to get a better view. A spark flew up, hitting him directly in the eye. Worse, being a bit short-sighted, he was wearing contact lenses and the red hot shard fused the lens to his retina.

Horrifically, when the bloke tried to take out his contacts, his retina came out too, blinding him for ever.

Overhaul

A bloke out in the suburbs of Bristol was doing a bit of DIY, painting the outside of his house. The house was a big thirties number with a drive out the front. He had hired some ladders for the job but they were just a little too short to reach the top of the walls.

Rather than wait 'til the next weekend and hire ladders of the correct size, he racked his brain for a way to avoid spending any more money. So he threw a rope over the roof and tied it to the bumper of his car, then went around and clambered up the back of the house, tying the rope round his waist.

Unbeknown to him, his wife decided to run some errands, got into the car, revved up and dragged her hapless hubby over the house and on to the front lawn with a thump.

The non-essential bane of modern parenting is the baby monitor, that cheap and not-so-cheerful development from the kids' walkie-talkie. It picks up passing mini-cab radio messages, and relays every gurgle and ambient noise within a hundred metres so it sounds like your baby's being choked by a bus driver, two dogs and a mad hissing maniac. More worryingly, unless you remember to switch off the thing when you're upstairs tending to baby, you may broadcast views you meant to remain private.

Baby talk

Some friends down in Brighton recently gave birth to a bouncing baby boy. As people do in this technological age they bought a baby intercom so they could listen to the little chap snoring and make sure he was all right up in his cot when they were downstairs.

It just so happened that they were out in the garden, as were all their neighbours, enjoying a well-earned rest in the hot summer sunshine, with the monitor switched on listening to the baby upstairs. Because they were quite a way down the garden from where the intercom was plugged in, they had it turned up to full volume.

The weather was lovely and hot and it seemed like they were on their own for the first time in ages. One thing led to another and they decided to take the opportunity to slip upstairs.

After a few minutes the woman had the feeling she could hear an echo of their passion, but thought nothing of it. Then she heard it again and realised the intercom was still on full and broadcasting their love-making to their startled neighbours outside and the world at large . . . she still gets knowing looks and the odd wink down her road even now.

Another couple had a similar nasty brush with modern parenting gadgetry. The mother's parents had come down to see the newly born offspring and completely overstayed their welcome.

The father of the nipper was particularly cheesed off with the situation, what with getting no sleep, having to be on his best behaviour in front of his priggish in-laws, having them eat him out of house and home, and getting an earful of their opinionated views on everything under the sun.

One evening they were sitting down to dinner when they heard the youngster start wailing over the monitor. The baby's mother went upstairs to see what was wrong, leaving the father to endure yet another lecture on perfect parenthood. The baby carried on crying, so the father made his excuses and went upstairs too. At the end of his tether, he stormed into the room and shouted 'God, I'm so sick of your mother! Why doesn't she sod off home,' before he realised the baby intercom was still turned on.

It was eerily quiet when they slunk back downstairs. They finished their meal in silence and, perhaps understandably, the next morning the in-laws were gone.

> Other phrases we know to have been broadcast:
> 'I don't care if it's his birthday party, Terry
> really is a pratt'; 'Hello gorgeous, you're so
> much prettier than that bug-eyed baby down-

stairs'; 'Golly, what a big tinkle!'.

It's not just making smells with a chemistry set,
or putting megavolts through door handles with
the help of an electronics kit, that can lead
youngsters into scientific scares, as this little
selection of adolescent antics shows:

A bridge too far

A young tearaway who'd just left school got in with a bad
crowd and started drinking heavily in the pubs and clubs
around Bolton. He'd always been a bit of a handful at school,
always cheeking the teachers, wagging it, and never wearing
school uniform.

One night after a particularly heavy session on the ale, he
was stumbling home with his mates, singing and shouting,
when the quantity of lager he'd imbibed made him desperate
to relieve himself.

Not being the shy type, he hopped up on to the parapet
of the bridge over the River Croal, unzipped his flies and
proceeded to empty his bursting bladder into the heavily
polluted river below.

While he was passing water, he was abusing passers-by,
waving and shouting and generally showing off, until in the
middle of his display he lost his footing and tumbled head
over heels into the orange foaming river below.

When his mate dragged him out he was dead — not from
drowning but, as the autopsy revealed, from toxic shock. . .

Course, these days, people report seeing salmon in the River Croal. Let's hope they're nothing like 'Mersey salmon'.

A shocking way to go

Not far from Harlow there's an electrified railway and during the long summer holidays some bored kids were messing about on the line. They'd kicked their ball over the fence and gone down on to the track to retrieve it.

One kid thought it'd be funny to whip out his todger and urinate on the line to see if it made steam. His mates stood back, the kid took aim, fired, and was frazzled in a second, winkle first.

The biker who lost his head

A bloke I know from Newcastle told me a story that happened to his sister back home. In a small country village just south of York in Yorkshire, some kids were fooling about on their motor bikes outside a local pub. The road was quite wide and parked opposite the pub was a rusty old farm trailer.

The lads were all about seventeen, and riding mopeds and bikes under 125cc with 'L' plates, because they hadn't passed their tests yet. They were showing off to a group of girls standing outside the pub by racing up the road behind the trailer, pulling wheelies and skidding on their sides out from under the edge of the trailer.

They took turns, going again and again, getting closer and

25

and closer to the trailer. The girls were all squealing with delight and egging the lads on to go faster and faster.

Unfortunately one biker, who was pulling a full throttle wheelie, lost control and slammed into the trailer. The back edge caught him full in the neck and snapped his head clean off, his severed helmet rolling across the road, coming to rest face-up in front of the gaggle of screaming girls.

> The Sky's the limit when it comes to ludicrous stories about the alleged properties of satellite dishes, but we've been told these with genuine fear of the dratted bowls. No doubt there will be many more emerging in the next few years, as seems to be the case with all new technology.

Doing the dishes

My uncle's mate from the bookie's is gadget mad. He was the first in his street with an 8-track, video recorder, Camcorder — you name it he's got it first. So it came as no surprise when satellite dishes appeared and he was straight down the shops, then straight up a wobbly old ladder screwing his purchase to the wall.

He's not really bothered about doing things properly, just likes to get jobs done and rush down the pub to carp on about them. It was a boiling day, and he was getting really hot and bothered putting it up. Finally, he got his reluctant wife to stand in front of the telly while he moved the dish to get optimum reception.

Eventually his wife shouted up to him that it was about as good as it had ever been, even though the bloke thought it seemed to be pointing far too low. So they drew the blinds and settled down to watch some Sky.

However, three hours later they heard a siren and some commotion. The house across the street had caught fire, and the neighbour came running across the road.

'You and your stupid gadgets!' he shouted. 'That bloody dish concentrated the sun and set light to our net curtains!'

Another DIY (Dish It Yourself) satellite enthusiast was up on his roof setting up his receiving equipment. He'd got the dish cheap from a bloke down the pub and there weren't any instructions. He was moving it about and shouting to his wife downstairs who had the telly on. Eventually the picture seemed okay and he came down off the roof to enjoy a top-notch evening's television entertainment. Everything was perfect at first but then every so often the picture began to flutter. He couldn't fathom out the problem 'til he was over the road at a neighbour's house and bragging about being wired up to satellite. He looked over to see two pigeons using the puddle in his badly adjusted dish as an impromptu bird bath.

Fax off and die

The invention of the fax has opened up a whole series of opportunities for pranksters. People can now transmit images of their faces, enlarged private parts or foul jokes directly into their victims' offices. There's fax junk mail and fax ads but to date nobody's invented fax food − although pizza down the phone can't be far off.

One company I've heard of got so sick of one of their suppliers sending stupid messages, junk faxes and anatomical details that they hit upon a novel method of revenge. They put together a fax loop, fed one end of a piece of paper with a skull and crossbones motif and the legend 'VIRUS' on it into the machine, taped it to the other end to form the loop, punched in the supplier's number and went home for the evening.

The suppliers arrived the next day to find a whole roll of wasted fax paper spewed out all over the floor.

> This next 'plane silly' set of stories circulate wherever pilots sit around sipping their Martinis. Pilots are notable for their alarming mistrust of technological innovations. Alarming, because these professional people's livelihoods, and the lives of all who travel with them, depend on the reliability of aircraft machinery. According to one former aviation engineer, every single plane has cracks in its wings; it's only when the cracks join up that you have to worry. With those thoughts in mind, read on. . .

Auto-pirate

According to an airline pilot friend today's big new jets, with all their hi-tech computer systems, aren't beyond the grip of gremlins.

He knows of a crew flying the Paris–London route who

approached the south coast of England on auto-pilot as usual, and passed over the navigation beacon that tells the computer where they are. But instead of steering them straight ahead as it should, the auto-pilot responded to the signal by banking sharply to port.

The crew immediately switched from auto to manual, and tried to steer back on line, but the computer wouldn't let them. The plane kept cruising to port, and by now quite concerned, the captain ordered the unplugging of the computer system, but still the controls failed to respond to his manipulation.

By now seriously worried, the captain noted they had nearly completed a full circle, and was about to radio that he was in difficulties when the plane once more passed over the navigation beacon below, the computer clicked, and the auto-pilot set a course straight ahead to Heathrow.

Jet scream

The same pal knows of another pilot who was doing a private job for some business people, running a luxury executive jet one-way from Newark in New Jersey to Norfolk, Virginia. The flight south passed without incident, and he was paid handsomely by the passengers. With time on his hands, the pilot decided to take a leisurely trip back on his own. Once he was airborne and on course, he switched to auto-pilot and put his feet up.

After a few minutes he remembered that his passengers had left some of their champagne in the rear galley and swiftly made his way there. A few glasses later he was walking back up to his cockpit, but to his annoyance he found that the cabin door had slammed shut.

The problem was that the jet was a modern one equipped with all the latest anti-terrorist devices – including cockpit doors that lock shut and can't be opened from the outside.

At first, the pilot wasn't too flustered: the plane was cruising on auto-pilot, and surely he'd be able to break the door down before he was over Newark? If not, he suddenly thought, it's running out of fuel and next stop the snowy wastes of Newfoundland for me.

So he set about breaking the door down with renewed urgency. A shoulder charge just hurt his shoulder. He couldn't kick it down. And in a panic he attacked it with some cutlery and glasses from the galley. Still he remained locked out of his cockpit and the controls.

Finally, after twenty minutes of agonising failure, he found a fire extinguisher and managed to smash the door in, just minutes before he would have flown over New York.

Jumbo leak

Another time in the seventies a Jumbo en route from Frankfurt to Rome was hijacked in mid-flight and the gun-toting terrorists demanded the plane be re-routed to Cuba. The flight crew stayed very calm, as did the passengers, even though the hijackers were screaming at them and waving their pistols around.

After a little while, when it was clear the flight crew were going to bluff them out, the terrorists – or freedom fighters, depending on your views – became very agitated. One of them started an altercation with a passenger, who bravely shouted back at him and squared up to him, fists raised. But the hijacker went spare and, in a moment of madness, fired his gun at the passenger, a huge German who obviously enjoyed his sausages and beer.

The bullet missed and shot through the plane's fuselage, causing a large hole and immediate decompression. The trigger-happy terrorist was sucked through the hole like a piece of spaghetti, and all the other passengers were ripped out of their seat by the force, as the plane spiralled out of control.

But the second person to be dragged towards the hole was the portly German. Luckily, he arrived at the gaping chasm bottom first — a part of his body amply equipped to stop him slipping any further — and completely plugged the gap. Normal oxygen supply was resumed, the plane came out of its spin and was able to land normally, and the remaining hijacker was arrested at the airport.

As for the hero, he was given a reward but treated for severe frostbite of the buttocks.

Superloo surprise

When the French superloo toilet — the space-age public lavs where you spend considerably more than a penny and the door flies open at crucial moments — was first introduced into this country, a man in Holland Park, London decided to make use of this twentieth-century marvel of modern technology. He settled himself down with his newspaper for a long sit. He was still reading the paper when his time ran out and the door sprang open, exposing him to the public gaze. Undaunted, he just stayed put.

It's worth reminding people that the superloo is self-cleaning, and at certain intervals the toilet bowl mechanically shunts back into a small hole in the wall to be automatically scrubbed and rinsed with boiling water. Sadly, that is exactly what happened on this occasion. The occupier was jammed in the mechanism, scalded and nearly cut in half. A passing bobby spotted a crowd round the convenience and raised the alarm, but the ambulance arrived too late. The man had bled to death.

What a way to go.

The technology involved in credit cards and cashpoints is impenetrable to lay people and has prompted a welter of implausible folklore, not always with a firm grounding in logic. It's a commonly held belief that with a bit of tape from a video and a PC, you can make your own digitally-imprinted cards. Newspaper financial pages suggest the boom area for this is the Far East. One paper, the *Guardian*, carried the story of a woman who had used someone else's credit card for nearly a year — and it wasn't even issued by the same bank. Our new dependance on the hole-in-the-wall banking system, tension at the humiliation of the screen publicly flashing up 'You must be joking' when you ask it for a tenner, and the threat that someone else might enjoy a new wardrobe, gallon of lager and a curry on the back of our stolen card, has created a fertile area for new Urban Myths. Some are even harder to swallow than the treacherous cards themselves:

Cashpoint Charlie

A jack-the-lad was out on the ale in London's Piccadilly area. When the pubs had closed, he strolled down to Charing Cross to catch his train home, but was gripped by the pressing need for sustenance. Checking his pocket, he found he had just about £1.80. It was a stark choice: home to Morden or a quarterpounder with all the trimmings. Then he remembered his flexible friend, his credit card!

So he swiftly nipped into a Burger Bar and had already started scoffing his flame-grilled patties when he reached the cashpoint. He put in his card, set his snack down next to the keypad, punched in his P.I.N. and waited for the cash to come rolling out. But the screen flashed up: 'SORRY, YOU HAVE USED THE WRONG PERSONAL NUMBER. DO YOU WISH TO TRY AGAIN?'

A bit flustered, he keyed in another number. Same message. Not a little fazed, he took stock and settled himself to try again. Convinced the first number was right and that he'd just keyed it in wrong, he carefully pressed the number again.

But when he finished, the screen flashed that his card had been retained, and the glass shield came grinding down, sadly locking away his delicious burger.

Fly-by-night

An office worker ran out of cash during an evening's drinking and, needing some cash for a taxi home, went to a hole-in-the-wall job.

He slipped in his card, the glass started to go up, and two startled pigeons flew out . . . .

Box of tricks

A colleague's friend's dad is something of an electronics boffin, and hit upon a fantastic little device. It was a tin of Old Holborn with lots of gadgetry inside.

When he put it on top of a fruit machine it looked innocent enough, but it altered the clicks of the machine and allowed the old fellow to pocket the £100 jackpot of any machine he wished. After cleaning out most of the big jackpots in Hounslow, he was banned from many places, but people didn't catch on about the tin.

After a good few months operating, though, he slipped up. He was at the Holiday Inn, Slough, working the machines as usual. But when he nipped off to the toilets, he accidentally left his jackpot tin on top of a fruit machine.

When he came out of the lavatory, the area was cordoned off, and he was collared by security. They'd mistaken his tin for a bomb, and his game was up.

The surprise package

A woman in her mid-thirties had suffered from a rare bowel

complaint and had to undergo pioneering surgery for the implanting of a mechanical sphincter.

The device allowed the bowels to be opened and closed by the passing of a magnet over a sensor placed in her chest, and although odd proved to be very effective, Until, that is, one day the unfortunate woman was jetting off for a fortnight in the sun, and happened to pass through the airport security scan.

It wasn't until she sat down in her window seat that she realised that airport scanners obviously use magnetism as well. . . .

Apparently shop security devices have been known to have a similar effect, usually on people leaving without paying 'by accident'.

Wrong ring

A friend of a former colleague told me about an incident that recently befell his boss on a train. He was feeling chuffed at claiming a four-seat table for himself and settled down to a nice quiet journey reading his book. The whistle blew and as the train lurched away, a loud, acne-ed yuppie trousered his way into the carriage and threw his bags down on the table, collapsed into the seat opposite, immediately brandished his portable phone and began a loud, oafish conversation — 'buy . . . sell . . . take a rain-check . . . hyper!' . . . — that sort of thing.

The quieter man couldn't believe his misfortune and tried to ignore the boorish city type, but he was so noisy, ringing

people up and rustling papers and shouting 'Yah. . . yah
. . . yah . . .' into the phone all the time, that the bloke
couldn't take any more and set off with his stuff for another
part of the train.

He'd just sat down when an old man opposite him went
pale and groaned. He was having a heart attack and collapsed
on the floor. The guard arrived as passengers tried to come
to the old gent's aid, and he explained that they'd have to
wait 'til the next station before they could phone as the train's
communication lines were down.

'I know someone with a phone!' said the bloke happily,
'we can ring ahead and have an ambulance waiting for him
at the station.'

So the guard, the bloke and some other concerned passengers marched triumphantly back down the carriage. The
yuppie was still in mid-conversation when the guard cut in
to explain the situation and ask him, as it was an emergency,
if they might have the use of his portable phone.

At first the yuppie waved them away as if he was busy,
still talking down the line. But when they persisted and got
increasingly agitated, he threw the phone down, went the
colour of beetroot and looking down mumbled, 'You can't.
It's only a fake phone.'

> Gas and electricity meters seem to throw down
> the gauntlet to some people and there are,
> allegedly, numerous ways to 'cheat' the system.
> Many have heard about the large round magnet
> from loudspeakers laid on top of the meter
> that's supposed to slow the dial's movement,
> or the hot pin piercing the plastic casing and

resting on the dial, slowing it down. Some people have even been foolish enough to try too hard and arrest the meter's progress altogether, forcing them to leave the heating on full on hot summer's days to avoid suspicion. The basic belief is 'there's always a loophole', and fiddling the meter is more mischievous than criminal. For example:

Life's a gas

Some people up the road from us were done for fiddling the gas. They'd made a mould, and were making 50p pieces from it out of ice − apparently both weigh roughly the same − and they'd got away with it for some time. They only got caught because one time when the Gas Board came to empty the meter, it was just full of water.

Charge of the light brigade

My old geography teacher told me about some friends of his who decided to get out of the rat race and moved to the Cornish coast. They bought a lovely ivy-covered cottage right out on a peninsular miles from any town. The only building nearby was the local lighthouse.

They had a fabulous time away from it all, without a care in the world. Until their electricity bill landed with a thud on the mat. The amount they owed was astronomical for such a tiny cottage. In fact, it ran into thousands of pounds.

Horrified, the couple rang the Electricity Board, who came

to investigate, and discovered that the light in the lighthouse was actually running off their domestic supply.

Mexican waves

A Mexican cook who'd been working in a run-down service station on the M4 for four months was taken ill one morning just as he was starting his shift.

He wasn't very reliable anyway, and when he complained of burning stomach pains, the supervisor only reluctantly agreed to let him drive to the nearest hospital some miles away, and warned him to be back soon, or he'd be given the big heave-ho.

After four hours, the cook still hadn't returned, so the maddened supervisor rang up the hospital where the Mexican had said he'd go, to see if he'd turned up there.

To his surprise, after a brief conversation with the casualty department, a specialist came on the phone and asked if the cook ever had to use a microwave.

'Yes, he does,' said the supervisor.

'And is it an old one?'

'Well, yes, one of the earlier models, why?'

'Stop using it immediately!' urged the consultant. 'The rays have been escaping, and your chef's kidneys have been cooked through.'

MYTHELLANEOUS

Technology

★ Credit cards' data and video tapes can be wiped by contact with: electric eels, lemon juice, mayonnaise, brown sauce, air terminal screening devices, the sparks under tube trains and scrap-yard electromagnets

★ Microwaves can make you sterile

★ All computers go wrong on Friday the 13th: it's a virus

★ Pacemakers go haywire in the anti-theft systems in shop doorways

★ People with pacemakers have to take rat poison to thin their blood

★ BT are working on contact lenses that relay messages

★ Every pilot has seen a UFO, but they're all sworn to secrecy. NASA is holding some aliens, but they won't let on because it would send the world into panic

★ Luminous divers' watches are radioactive

★ Sometimes when you're watching people on the TV, they can see you

CAR TROUBLE

Horsepower horseplay

'Two legs good, four wheels bad' (to nearly quote Orwell in *Animal Farm*) seems to be the maxim for this souped-up stupidity; or maybe 'Vorsprung durch cock-up'. What it boils down to is that anything other than a brand spanking new motor and a regular driver with a good grasp of where he or she's going, can only drive you round the bend — especially when you mean to go straight ahead. This high-octane injection of motorway madmen driven to despair, taxes the credulity to breaking point, where the most dangerous part of the car is the nut behind the wheel.

Cars? Wouldn't touch 'em with yours, mate!

Although the three-wheeled Reliant Robin is regarded by most discerning motorists as being economical, rust-free, nippy and a luxurious ride for a family of four, plentiful are the drivers who make jokes about it. Hence its nickname, the 'plastic pig' and all the rumours about the front wheel hitting a stone and flipping the whole thing right over. Some Robin owners themselves have combatted the myth with ingenuity — we know of one who was so fed up of honking boy-racers making jokes at his expense that he shoe-horned a V12 engine under his Robin's fibre-glass bonnet, and now haunts the streets of Liverpool, revving up at traffic lights next to any Porsche or flash GTi he can find.

The rocking Robin

At the other end of the country, a bloke from Chingford in Essex bought himself a Rover 3500 in the late seventies and customised it with all the extras: flared arches, metallic paint job, go-faster stripe and half-finished painting of a dragon on the side.

One day he was revving up at the lights as usual, aching for a burn-up, when a middle-aged husband and wife tootled up next to him in their Reliant Robin. To the boy-racer's surprise, the three-wheeler's driver began to rev up too. This was right up his street: 'No worries.'

But when the amber light flickered on the Reliant shot away like a bullet. The boy-racer was so shocked he nearly stalled trying to get away. He put his foot to the floor, but the plastic pig just kept accelerating away from him, peeling away towards the M1. By the time they hit the M1, they were doing well over a ton, and the souped-up Rover was feeling the pace; as they touched 110 mph, he sadly gave up the chase and the Robin stormed away into the distance.

Spark out

A fellow round the corner from us was setting out on a shopping trip with his wife one Saturday morning. They got in the car, turned the key but it wouldn't start. The bloke opened the bonnet, had a look, and noticed an oil leak. So he set about repairing the car while his missus went shopping on her own.

A couple of hours later, the wife returned laden with bags, and was just walking up the drive when she spotted her husband's legs poking out from under the car. Feeling a bit frisky, she ran her hand up the inside of his thigh, and gave him a loving tweak. Then she went inside to put away the groceries.

But when she got in the house, she found her husband in the kitchen drinking a cup of tea. They both rushed outside to find the mechanic still lying under the car, unconscious from banging his head when he was intimately groped.

New constructions often provoke an interest that soon develops into notoriety and ends, inevitably, in myth. Apart from the endemic stories of 'grasses' from London's gangland East End being set in the concrete pillars, the M25 has already conjured up an unrivalled notoriety. With its tales of city yuppies and their early-hours racing, its grid-locked hold-ups with no obvious cause, and its seemingly inbuilt obsolescence, it is a particularly good example. There's nothing very new about the Urban Myths surrounding the M25, just that its orbital quality seems to add a new twist to the story. For example. . .

Up north

An elderly London couple decided, after years of putting it off, to drive north and visit their daughter and son-in-law in Leeds.

So they got their old Ford Anglia out of the garage, washed the accumulated dirt and cobwebs off it, and set out.

They were driving along the motorway for six hours, but still hadn't seen a signpost for Leeds. Puzzled, they resolved to ask someone in a service station.

'You're in South Mimms, mate, five miles out of London.' They'd neglected to turn off the M25.

Auf wiedersehen Trabbie

Just as the Berlin wall was crumbling, an 'Ossie' (the German for an 'Easterner') in his thirties who'd long held aspirations to become a rock star decided the time had come to make his decisive move. So he packed all his belongings in his knackered old Trabant and headed off for Liverpool, home of the Beatles, to make his name as a musician.

It was a nightmare journey, and for long parts of it he was only sustained by his dream of a new life. He had to queue virtually all day at the Austrian border having made his way through Hungary, and he grew nervous when the border guards scoured his passport. But he and his trusty Trabant made it through the tattered Iron Curtain to the West and chugged triumphantly across southern Europe.

In France, though, he hit more trouble. He had a minor crash, and the Trabbie's exhaust worked loose, so that it was making even worse noises than before. At Calais, he had to pay someone to bodge the car, which after such a huge journey was on its last legs.

Having bought his ferry ticket, he was virtually penniless — he'd been stung when he tried to change his currency back in Austria. But on the boat's deck, with the white cliffs of Dover ahead, his spirit swelled and his hopes rose.

Disembarking at Dover, the Ossie drove down the ramp and heard a clunk. The Trabbie's exhaust had finally lopped off with a clang. Still determined to fulfil his dream, the Ossie headed for London, next stop Merseyside.

He was chugging along fine until just south of the capital, when he encountered the dreaded M25, which wasn't on his old map at all.

By now the Trabbie was puffing out great plumes of black smoke, and he was limping along noisily in the nearside lane, swerving around as he tried to read the map for directions. To no avail.

He drove around the M25 for two hours, until the shabby

Trabant drew the attention of Highway Patrol. They took one look at his death-trap car and fired questions at him. Unfortunately, the only English he spoke was learnt from Beatles songs, and was precious little help in this situation.

Getting no sense from him, and noting that he had no money, the police arrested him, and within days the Ossie was deported back to East Germany, heartbroken. Meanwhile, the rusting, abandoned Trabbie can still apparently be seen in the bushes next to the M25.

> This particularly long and uninteresting myth
> is really just an update on earlier refugee
> stories. Previous incarnations involving Pales-
> tinians seem even more implausible.

The driving dog

A fella I worked with reckons his American uncle was banned from driving for being over the limit, but was mad on cars and liked his drink. So he bought an automatic and taught his St Bernard dog to drive. The dog would steer, and he would manipulate the other controls using a driving school dual-control facility. He even applied for a provisional driver's licence for the dog under the name Henry St Bernard as a joke. But it paid off, and the dog became something of a familiar and popular figure in the small town, driving his master to the shops or a bar. After a little while, though, the highway police stopped and arrested them. But there was such a public outcry that the charges were dropped and the man got off with a simple warning. Henry the dog didn't get off so lightly: he was fined $50 for driving after dark on a provisional licence. . .

Inertia reel sick-belt

Where I used to work they had a company car that anyone in the department could drive. It was a powerful three-litre Capri. On one Friday night two of the lads from work borrowed it to go to a posh client's party to the west of London on the Thames.

They had a great time, drinking and dancing 'til the small hours, until one of them felt the worse for wear and they both decided to leave. Heading back home, the sickly one's condition was made worse by the driver's recklessness, and soon he was vomiting all over the place, but mostly down his silk shirt.

The car was returned to the pool after a weekend spent cleaning and valeting it. Nothing was said.

Until the next week, when the stuck-up boss borrowed it. He decided to take his blue-rinse mother out to a garden party, and pulled up outside, beeping the horn gently. The stiff old dear tottered out in her Sunday best clobber.

She got in the car, settled herself down and, being safety conscious, pulled the seat belt across her, only to be streaked with a sash of whiffy, stale spew.

Dad's pullover

The manager of our local wine bar was a little the worse

for wear one afternoon and driving through London in his pristine mimosa yellow 1964 Ford Zephyr.

As he was passing Buckingham Palace, he could see a motorbike cop right behind him. The cop flashed him to pull over, and he thought he'd had his chips. He wound down his window as the policeman approached him, steeling himself for a nabbing, which would mean the loss of his licence — he was already up to his points limit.

'What's the problem, officer?' he asked nervously.

'Nothing,' beamed the young copper, 'it's just that my dad had one just like this!'

MYTHELLANEOUS

Cars

★ Sawdust in the gearbox makes it quieter

★ Kicking the tyres is a fine way to suss out a second-hand motor

★ Stolen cars are often two different motors welded together

★ There's a red Porsche with the registration number 'PEN15'

★ A Cadillac worker built his own car from little bits stolen over the years

★ Cars built on Fridays are always very dodgy

★ People often put sugar in a rival's petrol tank to clog the engine

★ Kids blow gaskets by shoving a spud up the exhaust; once one shot out and killed a dog

★ Sticking vinyl stripes on your car makes it go faster

★ When you're in your car, people can't see you picking your nose

★ Old Citroëns can't be wheel-clamped because of their low suspension

★ Rolls-Royces never get parking tickets

THE LONG ARM OF THE LAW

Arresting tales of brushes with authority

Felonious frolics with a perverse sense of justice are the hallmark of this, the section with retribution under its jurisdiction. Drink-drivers, gullible accomplices, oddly endowed burglars and saucy students in collar-feeling confrontations that may prove the law's an ass, but it's mostly their asses that get kicked when they're bang to rights. As far as myth-lovers are concerned, any old legal yarn is a fair cop, and society is definitely to blame. Pass the bracelets, slap 'em in the slammer for a long stretch of the imagination . . .

Double-take

A couple in Surbiton woke up one morning to find that their car had been stolen from outside their house, and promptly reported it to the police. Then later the same day, they returned home from work to see the car back again, with an envelope under a windscreen wiper.

Inside, a note made profuse apologies for the 'borrowing' of their motor. The man who wrote it explained he didn't have a car himself, and his wife had gone into labour with their first baby. So he hoped they didn't mind too much that he'd taken their car without consent to run her to the hospital, as an emergency measure.

To soften the blow, he'd enclosed two tickets for a West End show at the weekend, which they were chuffed to use.

However, when they got home after the show, they found that the cheeky crook had taken advantage of their absence and robbed their entire house of its contents.

To add insult to injury, they later found out that their car had been used for a robbery on the very day it had disappeared.

Fat filly foils felony

I've never found out exactly who this happened to, but I have my suspicions that it was a teacher friend of the woman that told me.

Anyway, the woman involved in the story was extremely large, stout, portly, big-boned, call it what you will. One day she popped down to her building society in Exeter and was just squeezing through the revolving doors when she noticed there was a hold-up in progress.

The two inexperienced bandits threw everyone into a blind panic by waving shotguns around and screaming at the customers to get out, including the large lady. They proceeded to force the staff to hand over all the cash, then told them to get down and stay down on the floor 'til they were well away.

But when they turned to make their getaway they found the big lass sweating and in a right fluster, stuck fast in the revolving doors. The villains grabbed her and tried to force her through, then pull her out, but she was jammed and so were the doors. Shooting her wouldn't have done much good, and there was no other way out. They were trapped, like trapped rats in a rat trap for rats.

A few minutes later the police arrived − complete with a man carrying a blow-torch to free the humiliated lady − and arrested the crooks.

Ironically, although the lady was in all the papers and offered a large reward by the building society, she was too embarrassed to attend the presentation ceremony.

The one-legged bandit

A friend moved from inner-city Birmingham (who wouldn't?) to the sprawling suburbs; a nice little semi that needed a bit of work, especially in the garden. As soon as he was in he set to it, and laid some cement to make a patio. That night, drained by his day of toil, he went out for the evening to the local pub.

When he got home he was dismayed to find he'd had a break-in, but couldn't find anything stolen. Puzzled, he called the police. An officer arrived and scoured the place for clues, inside and out. It was from the garden that he called the man, saying he'd found something very suspicious, and pointed his torch at the patio.

Curiously there was a single row of footprints across the wet cement and they were *all* clearly left footed.

Rag week roadworks

As we all know most students are right prankers, and one bunch sorted out a cracking wheeze for rag week.

They divided into two bunches. One lot went to see some navvies who were about to dig up the road and tipped them off that a bunch of their mates were going to turn up later dressed as coppers, for a rag week prank. They said their mates would tell them to stop what they were doing and clear off, by order. The workers thanked them for the tip-off and promised they'd have a surprise of their own ready.

The other bunch went to the police station pretending to shop their mates who they said were dressed up as road workers putting cones down and disrupting traffic. Right, said the desk sergeant, we'll send some of the lads down there sharpish.

When the genuine police met the genuine road gang, both thinking the others were students, there was not a little confusion and according to some sources an almighty dust-up.

[For more undergraduate uproar, *see* **Friends and Relations** and **Under the Knife**]

The majority of urban legends in this legit section involve cars. It's ironic that although in the cop movies it's always seen as the ultimate humiliation to be put on traffic duty after being taken off a case, many civvies would like to be in their position just to have a go on one of those huge BMW bikes.

Another abiding myth is that if you can just get home you'll be okay — the 'Englishman's home is his castle'. But it's easily stormed by the motorised boys in blue . . .

[*See also* **Demon Drink**]

Blue light spells danger

A workmate's uncle was driving home one evening along a busy urban ring road. The thing is, he was so drunk he could hardly stand, and he shouldn't have been sitting in a car, let alone driving one. He was crawling along the inside lane of the dual carriageway trying not to draw attention to himself. But he was going so slowly (with the occasional sidelong weave) that his driving had the opposite effect, and he was soon pulled over by the law.

They took one look at his rolling oyster eyes and caught one whiff of his breath, and 'suggested' he abandon his car and accompany them to the station. They were just about to take him away when two cars had a smash on the other side of the central reservation. The coppers warned the inebriated uncle to stay put and dashed over.

But spotting his chance to make his escape during the commotion, he jumped into action. Making sure the coppers didn't see him, he sped home as fast as he could. He drove straight into the garage and ran inside, telling his startled wife: 'If the police come round, I've been ill all day with a cold, haven't been out, haven't used the car and I'm asleep in bed, okay?' Then he picked up a bottle of whisky and wobbled off to bed.

Half an hour later the police turned up. The wife answered the door, and blurted out, 'He's been ill all day, hasn't used the car, and is asleep now,' before they'd even asked anything. 'In that case you won't mind if we take a look in your garage, madam,' said one officer, and she sheepishly handed over the keys.

As they opened the door, the wife gasped. There, to the officers' obvious satisfaction, was a police car, with the radio blaring out and the blue light still flashing away.

Number plate giveaway

A bloke I know who's a bit of a drinker was at another friend's party just round the corner. He was hitting the sauce quite hard until the early hours of the morning, by which time he was several sheets to the wind. Too drunk to walk, he decided, against everyone's advice, to drive home, saying, 'My Datsun drives itself.'

It was winter and raining pretty hard, but despite being totally inebriated, he was making pretty good progress home until he swerved round a corner and smashed into a stationary vehicle. Despite the horrendous crash, no lights went on in any of the houses down the street, so the bloke reversed as fast as he could and sped away, his heart racing.

He got home, ran inside and fell asleep fully clothed on his bed.

Half an hour later, there was a knock at the door. The drinker staggered downstairs and gingerly opened the door. It was the police.

'Sorry to bother you, sir,' said one rozzer, while the other one examined the damage on his car parked outside. 'Did you by any chance crash your car into another vehicle just round the corner from here?'

'Err, yes,' stammered the bloke. 'But how did you know?'

'You left this embedded in the front grille, sir,' said the officer, producing the battered number plate from his car.

Backwards in the fast lane

The boss of a friend had been out in town one night living it up in a champagne bar. He stumbled out into his Porsche in the wee small hours and set off home via the M25. There were no other cars about and the fat cat put his foot to the floor, soon reaching a ton.

He was enjoying himself so much that he missed his turning, and, this being a motorway, the next junction was miles away. Screeching to a halt, and checking to see if anything was behind in the dark, he decided to risk backing up to his turning in the outside lane.

He slammed the car into reverse, stamped down hard on the accelerator and careered backwards. Then SMASH! An

Escort XR3i had ploughed straight into him. The police arrived immediately and rushed up to the other driver.

The Porsche driver was fretting, thinking he'd be breathalysed and get a life ban or something. After a short time one of the officers walked towards him. He felt his heart flutter.

'Scuse me, sir, but have you had a few jars tonight at all?' asked the officer.

'Yes, I have to admit I have had a little to drink,' confessed the driver, expecting the worst.

Then the officer leaned forward conspiratorially and said, 'I shouldn't worry about it mate, the other driver's so ratted he thinks you were reversing in the fast lane.'

'This is a pick-up!'

A workmate's son is a motorcycle courier. One day he received a call for a wait-and-return job to go from an address in King's Cross to a large bank in the middle of London, and back to King's Cross again. The biker nipped through the heavy traffic to the pick-up place and collected a small brown envelope and a holdall, which he put in his pannier, and headed off for the bank.

He arrived at the bank, propped up his bike and went inside, handing over the envelope to a cashier as directed. Within seconds of the woman reading the note, alarms went off all over the joint, and the place was crawling with gun-toting security guards.

The courier, standing in his full garb — leathers, skid lid and radio stuttering away — was so stunned he couldn't speak. Later, in the police station, they showed him the note that had been in the envelope.

It read: 'Fill the bag with money. I've got a gun, and I'm not afraid to use it.'

Get the picture

A friend who's a photographer in one of London's swankiest areas, swinging Chelsea, told me about a mate of his in the same line of work and who was involved in a most regrettable occurrence.

The photographer had been working late on an advertising shoot, for a well-known diamond necklace company. He'd been snapping the sparklers all day and well into the evening, and was feeling pretty bushed until the art director on the shoot suggested a quick snifter.

Taking the diamonds with them for safety's sake, they tootled off to the local boozer for a few jars. A few too many – by last orders the photographer was more than merry. He waved the art director off in his cab and caught the last tube home.

To his detriment, he fell straight asleep, missed his station and was woken by the guard at the end of the line. He didn't have the foggiest where he was, out in the sticks somewhere, and there was no train back, so he decided to hitch back to London. He was trudging along a deserted country road in the drizzle, when he heard a car behind him coming up fast.

He stuck out his thumb and it skidded to a halt. It was two young lads driving a souped-up Cortina, lit up like a Christmas tree. As he clambered in they were revving like mad. He scarcely had the door shut before they screeched off and he tumbled into a heap in the back.

From nowhere, there was a police car behind them giving chase. The lads put their foot down. The photographer was getting thrown all over the place as the lads screeched round corners on two wheels, hotly pursued by the wailing police car, until the Cortina hurtled off the road, rolled over and over and over and hit a tree in a field.

The photographer came round with police torches flashing in his eyes. His case had burst open, the upturned car was strewn with precious jewels and the lads were nowhere to be seen.

It was all the photographer could do to slur drunkenly, 'It's not how it looks, ossifer, I can explain!'

MYTHELLANEOUS

The law

★ The police can't arrest you for drink-driving if you make it home and have a swig of whisky (keep a miniature on your dashboard)

★ If the police can't keep up with you, you can't get done for speeding

★ If you make a Masonic sign in court, you can get off any charge; some murderers have only been hanged because they made the sign too late

★ Supergrasses always have plastic surgery, are given loads of cash and get set up with a new identity and loads of birds in the Caribbean

★ If you get stopped by the police and say you're a judge's son, they let you off every time

★ Tramps try their best to get arrested to have a warm bed for the night

DEMON DRINK

Tales of the tipple that topples

As if people aren't capable of getting in enough trouble
without alcohol's helping hand. As this selection proves, once
liquor's involved, a cocktail of confusion is almost inevitable,
especially if the victim isn't used to its debilitating ways,
or insists on driving home on a belly-full of lager. Drink
just can't seem to handle people. When it comes to work,
rest or play and alcohol, it's better not to mix it. Above all,
this chapter is grist to the mill of those who say that work
is the curse of the drinking classes . . .

The office party and Mr Byrite

A straight-laced, hen-pecked office worker in London's West End attended his Xmas office party in the afternoon, but rather overdid it with the drinks, made a complete nonce of himself and ended up being violently sick all over his clothes.

Realising that his garb was ruined, but not wanting to miss his train to Brighton, he nipped down to Mr Byrite on Oxford Street for some new clobber.

In the shop, he spent about two minutes choosing the stuff, throwing it in a pile on the till as he went, and then hurriedly paid for it.

He just about caught his train, and rushed straight for the toilet, tearing off his stinking damp trousers, shirt and jacket and recklessly throwing them out of the train window.

Then he opened the bag to put on his new clothes, and discovered, to his dismay, that all he had in there was some socks, a T-shirt and two cardigans.

Dead man's handle

During the Second World War, a bomb landed directly on a Cardiff pub and flattened it to rubble. The ARP were at the scene promptly, and asked eyewitnesses if any people were inside at the time of impact.

After some discussion, some of the locals worked out that the bomb landed dead on six-thirty, which was exactly the time old Bill used to always turn up at the pub for his habitual pint of Brains Light. So they all set about rapidly moving the rubble. A few minutes later, though, they were shocked to discover the outside door handle — with old Bill's gnarled hand still attached to it.

The man from Dudley

A coach party from the Midlands was on a day trip to the Welsh seaside town of Barmouth. They'd had a fabulous time: the beach, bingo, fish and chips and a few drinks.

As they crossed the pub car park back to the coach they found a bloke who judging by his accent was from Dudley. He was really drunk so they helped him on board. He fell asleep immediately, snoring loudly.

When they arrived in the Black Country, they woke him up and said, 'We're nearly back in Dudley, now, mate.'

The bloke jumped up with a start. 'Dudley? But I've only just started two weeks holiday in Barmouth with the wife and kids!'

Put it down to the late hours, the adrenalin-pumping pressure or the abundance of wedge, but there must be something special about the 'square mile' of London and its big-bang city drinkers. Always first with a sick joke (in both senses), and always, it seems, last to the train station. In sickness and in wealth, the City's a fertile ground for urban myths:

The sickly city slicker

A friend who works in the City told me about a colleague of his who's a real yuppie commuter.

He'd been out after work, celebrating heavily in a wine bar all night, and as usual had to run to catch the last train home. He was there in his double-breasted pin-stripe suit and light trench coat with his portable phone and Filofax safely in his leather briefcase. The train was packed with late revellers and other officer workers going home and the swaying and lurching of the ancient rolling stock was making him feel more than a bit queasy. There was a sudden jolt and he knew he was going to throw up, so he opened the briefcase and nearly filled it to the brim.

The next day he woke up with an appalling hangover, remembering with a shudder about his case and that his wife was downstairs making his sandwiches. He leapt out of bed, ran downstairs and burst into the kitchen just in time to see his wife picking up his case.

'Don't open that!' he blurted out.

'Why?' she asked, ignoring him and opening it, only to find it was completely empty. Someone else's wife must have got a nasty shock that morning . . .

Terminally drunk

Another City suit known to my chum was also partial to a spritzer or two. He also often used to catch the last train home so as to maximise his drinking time, but he nearly always fell asleep, missed his stop, and ended up right out on the south coast, at the end of the line.

He worked out the only solution to his problem was to buy an extremely expensive all-singing, all-dancing top-dollar swanky alarm watch, which he set to go off and rouse him just before his station. Unfortunately, the next night the watch went off on his wrist but failed to wake him from his intoxicated slumber, and he ended up at the seaside again.

So in desperation after the next night's session he boarded the train and hung his flash chronometer off his ear and settled down to sleep.

Sadly, he woke up in the small hours to the sound of seagulls again. Even worse, the watch had vanished . . .

Keep it up your sleeve

Another City-type who works for a big investment bank had been out entertaining a client. They'd hit all the high spots, happy hours, Karaoke bars and strip joints. The champers had been flowing like water. Totally paralytic, the banker caught the last tube home.

It was quite full, so he was strap-hanging, his head lolling against his arm. Suddenly he knew he was going to be sick, but the packed tube was in the middle of a tunnel and he couldn't wait. He took the only available option: put his cuff to his mouth and threw up down the inside of his raincoat sleeve.

Sadly, he didn't remember about this the next day until, spry in his freshly dry cleaned suit, he picked up his coat from the back of the door and put it on.

Just as prevalent as the city drinking tales are those of rural inebriates, but in keeping with the different nature of things in the country, the stories feature far more animals and far less trains. The rustic raconteur must be driven by the slower pace of life, the tranquillity — and the sheer boredom — to come up with tales involving plenty of drinking and plenty of pranks:

The night stalker

A friend of my dad's always drank in the same boozer down a leafy country lane, and was in the habit of taking a piece of meat with him in his pocket.

Every night he'd stagger out of the bar, slightly the worse for wear, take out the morsel of meat and hold it above his head. An owl that roosted nearby would swoop silently down, snatch the meat and fly off to a tree to eat it, every time.

One night he left the pub after a particularly heavy sesson and had an overwhelming urge to relieve himself there and then, so he staggered over to a suitable bush and did so. Obviously confused, the ravenous owl swooped down, talons poised, for its usual portion of flesh . . .

Which just goes to show it's not always the early bird that catches the worm.

A stable environment

A friend who lives out in the sticks in Lincolnshire told me of a strange occurrence down at their local.

One of the regulars, an elderly tippler, used to travel down to the pub using an old-fashioned clapped-out horse and cart. He was usually five sheets to the wind when he left the ale house and was always crashing into cars in the car park and causing damage to walls and hedges. Not only that but his horse regularly left steaming booby traps right outside the pub's front door for the locals to tread in.

All in all, the old man and his antiquated transport were very unpopular. One night, the regulars decided to teach him a lesson. At closing time the old drunk came out to find the horse and cart had disappeared, so he set off walking, swaying from side to side.

When he did eventually get home he found his horse and the cart already there, impossibly crammed into his tiny cottage's front room. The carpet was ruined.

Shire indulgence

The same friend told me about another local character in the next village way out in the middle of nowhere. This bloke was a farmer who liked a drink. Living as he did a long way from the nearest hostelry he used to ride down to the pub on a horse — he was banned for drink driving. The locals reckoned the nag knew the way better than the inebriated old soak, as he was often drunk on home-made cider even before he set off for the pub.

One night the farmer had arrived on his pony and was propping up the bar as usual, when some of the regulars decided to play a trick on him, and plied the horse with a bucketful of beer. The paralytic farmer eventually waddled out of the snug and mounted his steed. The poor beast was quite sozzled and immediately began to stagger, drunkenly weaving about all over the village, causing untold havoc until the local bobby was forced to act.

The poor old farmer was charged with being drunk in charge of an even drunker horse and banned from riding. Apparently, he now goes to the pub on his prize bull to prevent interference.

Yer 'tis

This myth is still told by locals all over the West Country as a warning to 'grockles' (tourists) about the strength and potency of the cider or scrumpy produced in the vicinity.

'You want to be careful drinking the scrumpy in here. Four big strong farm labourers, huge great blokes, used to come in here all the time and drink pint after pint of farmhouse scrumpy. They'd often down ten pints or more every night. Most folks can't even manage four and still walk. Anyway, because it's so acidic, it rotted their stomachs. They all got cancer and died, all of them, one right after the other . . .'

MYTHELLANEOUS

Drinking

★ If you get drunk on Pernod, a pint of water in the morning makes you tipsy again

★ Sunshine exaggerates the effects of alcohol

★ Pub clocks are always five minutes fast

★ It is possible to drink yourself sober

★ Hangover cures: a good fry-up; raisins; egg and a Guinness; 'hair of the dog'

★ Hangover prevention: drink some milk to 'line your stomach'; don't mix grains, or the grape and grain; have a curry

★ You always get home somehow after a session

★ Being drunk makes you more gentle in bed

★ It's always the kebab that makes you sick, never the eleven pints of lager

★ No matter how much money you go out with for a booze-up, you always end up with slightly less than you need for the night bus home

★ Once you've had the fatal first slash, you'll be visiting the pub toilet all night

★ You generally find a big beetle in the bottom of African beer

FOOD FOR THOUGHT

Awful à la carte anecdotes

If there's one thing bigoted Brits don't like someone messing about with, it's their daily bread, and any foreign deviation from meat and two veg is regarded as the devil's own dumplings. But if the stomach is the best avenue to a man's heart, the fear of foreign (even animals') bodies or other unwarranted additives is a tempting little side road. Our appetite for stomach-churning, gut-busting stories is voracious, and half-baked myths such as this are spiced up, told with a special relish and are always on the conversational menu . . .

Thinking of going on a diet? Read on . . .

Dog's dinner

A large man from Rochdale bought a family size steak and kidney pudding, steamed it carefully, heated up some mushy peas, fried up some chips and set the table.

He'd practically scoffed the lot, washed down with a good strong cuppa, when swooping for his last forkful his utensil clattered against something metallic. Fishing around, he hooked out a strange metal disc on a ring.

It was a dog's tag, with the name 'Lucky' engraved on it.

Chinese poodle

A wealthy husband and wife went out for a meal at a busy new local Chinese restaurant, taking their pet poodle with them.

During the meal, their pampered pooch kept whining, so the woman beckoned to one of the waiters, who came over to her. She asked if it might be possible for him to find something for her dog to eat so he didn't feel left out.

The waiter obviously didn't understand her, so she said the same again, only louder and slower. He shook his head and grunted.

So the woman, who had spent some time travelling round the Empire when Britain had one, set about explaining her wish using hand gestures, pointing to the poodle, then her plate and then her stomach, and making 'yum yum' sounds.

The waiter's face lit up and he indicated he understood. So he leant forward and took the dog's lead from the woman's hand and led the frisky poodle away.

Twenty minutes later, the waiter returned the poodle to the

couple's table. Though to their horror, it was now roasted on a silver plate with an orange in its mouth and all the trimmings.

This myth is often told with more than a hint of racism about the local Chinese or Indian restaurant, and plays on the Anglo-Saxon's deep-seated fear of anything foreign, especially 'spicy' food. Variations on the theme include:

'The local Chinese near us was raided by the police and environmental health, and they closed it down because in the freezer they found half-eaten Alsatians hanging up and cats' carcasses in the waste skips . . . '

Which is often followed by, 'Well, they eat dogs in China don't they', 'they eat Derby winners for dinner in France', and 'the Italians make pies out of our migrating songbirds', or the ever-green:

'You know in Hong Kong they have special tables with holes in that close round a monkey's head, and they chop the top off its skull and eat its brains . . .'

Then there's the rejoinder, 'Well, if it tastes okay, I'm not complaining.' It's the *knowing* that's nasty, and always has been, ever since Sweeney Todd introduced his new line in pies. Talking of mystery ingredients . . .

Southern-fried rodent

A friend had gone to the local fleapit to see the latest all-

American Hollywood blockbuster. Feeling a bit peckish, she dashed into a well-known fast food outlet and bought a carton of southern American-style fried chicken and took it into the cinema.

As she was a bit late the lights were already down when she settled herself at the back. The movie began and she started to tuck into her grub, munching her way through the entire film.

When the lights came up she looked down into the carton and saw, to her horror, the back leg and tail of what was unmistakeably a large fried rat.

Pie-eyed

A friend of a friend's family were eating a shop-bought shepherd's pie with chips and beans for their tea. They'd often had pies before from the same shop and enjoyed the tasty convenience of this ready meal, which left them more time to live their lives.

The daughter was tucking in with gusto when her fork hit something hard. Thinking it was a bit of gristle, she peeled back the browned and seasoned potato-effect crust and looked in.

To her consternation, nestled in the mince was a human glass eye staring right back at her.

Handy loaf

Some people down our street bought a loaf of sliced bread, but when they opened it they were shocked to find a human finger in the middle of the loaf.

Oddly, although the bread was sliced, the digit was uncut. Even stranger, no one at the bakery had reported an accident.

Nowt taken out

A Yorkshire family was sitting down to tea and slicing up the bread for chip butties. Father cut a slice that seemed to have a small black mark in the centre. The mark got bigger with each slice, until the stunned family could gradually make out the shape of a dead mouse baked into the loaf.

An offal experience

A friend's mother had left it a bit late to sort out the family's evening meal, and not having anything to hand, she dashed down to the local butcher's.

To her concern, they'd sold everything apart from some dodgy-looking liver that was definitely on the turn, but they said she could have it cheap, so she took it. She put her bargain in the fridge and went about her chores.

A few hours later she opened the fridge to start the tea and to her horror, the 'liver' had crawled up the side of a milk bottle.

Sick as a . . .

A block of flats round the corner from us was in a pretty bad state of repair. It was infested with cockroaches and silverfish and permanently damp. The residents complained 'til they were blue in the face but nothing was really done to improve matters, until eventually all the block's inhabitants fell ill with stomach bugs.

Everyone was extremely sick, and no one could explain why the illness was so localised, until Environmental Health found seventeen dead pigeons in the block's water tank.

[*See also* Vatman, **Urban Classics**]

Bistro bog bother

A woman friend of a friend went out to a snobby bistro in Chelsea with her new escort (a bloke, not a car), but was struck halfway through the meal by the pressing need to pass a motion. So she asked for the lav, and was directed down some passages to a tiny, decrepit water closet, where she gratefully relieved herself.

Come flushing time, however, she was mortified at three things. Firstly, her log was huge. Secondly, someone was knocking on the door to get in. Thirdly, and worst, the cistern was empty and she couldn't flush the toilet.

Quickly, she decided to fish out the sizeable stool in toilet paper and throw it through the small window. This she did, and returned sheepishly to her table.

At the end of a smashing evening, her boyfriend helped her on with her coat and they stepped outside into the moonlight, but after a few paces she lost her footing, ending up on the pavement, having slipped on some 'brown stuff'.

The presence of toilet paper left her in no doubt that she was the victim of her own waste disposal technique.

Russian bangers

Apparently, a recent consignment of sausages on sale in the Russian Republic was snapped up by hungry Muscovites the minute they arrived on the shelves.

Too late, the authorities tried to withdraw them, warning that they were made up of '70 per cent rat fur'.

Keep it under your hat

Before the fall of Communism in the old Soviet Union food was often in short supply, especially meat products – unlike today.

In a supermarket in Moscow, a woman, who had been standing for hours in a typically lengthy checkout queue, collapsed. The concerned staff rushed to loosen her clothing and discovered that she had been trying to steal a frozen chicken, by smuggling it out under her large fur hat.

In a peculiar twist of fate, the pilfered poultry had frozen her brain solid and she was quite dead.

Pea brain

An elderly couple we know from the genteel part of Enfield in north London had been married for forty-five years, but with little in common.

They'd seen their two children grow up and have families of their own, and had gradually settled into a kind of unspoken hatred of each other's domestic ways, which they both played up to. But still they kept up the pretence that it didn't matter to either of them. It was a quietly seething battle that had worsened over the twenty-five years since the kids had quit the nest.

The bloke's most annoying habit, the one that secretly riled his wife the most (and he knew it) was that whenever she cooked him peas for tea (which was often), he would always manage to leave just one of them on the spotless plate.

For four decades the woman would look across the table, see the knife and fork lined up neatly with a solitary pea next to them, and catch her husband's inane smirk. He thought he was so funny.

Then a few years ago, she finally cracked. She cooked fish, chips and peas for tea, and, as usual, her sickening spouse left one pea on his plate. But this time, when he looked over to her with his smug, self-satisfied grin, she launched herself across the table, grabbed the pea from the plate and splatted it right in the middle of his big bald pate with a slap.

Peanut

A health visitor my brother knows used to regularly visit an old geezer in Edmonton, north London. Every time she went round, he'd fix up something for her to eat: cake and biscuits, or sandwiches. He so looked forward to her visits.

One day, he was a little ill, so she popped round to see

him unannounced. He was very pleased to see her, but was flustered because he had no food to offer her apart from a little bag with a few peanuts in it.

She picked out a handful and munched on them. The old fellow told her to finish them, so she ate another load.

'I can't eat the peanuts anyway, they get stuck in my falsies,' he explained, adding, 'I just suck the chocolate off them.'

> Shades of Will Hay, Moore Marriott and a bag
> of boiled sweets about that one:
> Hay takes a red one, and old man Marriott says,
> 'D'you like the red ones? I always spit 'em out
> and put them back in the packet.'

Fruity salad

The Mambo Inn, a club in Brixton, London, famous for its tropical music and cosmopolitan crowd, was treated to a spectacle one night. A macho Latin-American type was creating a bit of a stir on the dancefloor, as much for the inviting bulge in his tight leather trousers as his luscious lambada steps. But after about an hour of sensual movement, the sweat-soaked demon dancer suddenly fainted and collapsed in the middle of the dancefloor, to gasps. Luckily a doctor was at hand, and he was soon aware that the problem was a serious obstacle to the victim's blood circulation. There were more gasps when the doctor undid the man's flies, reached in and . . . pulled out a huge cucumber that had stopped the blood flow in the man's thighs. Cucumber Man was never seen at the Mambo again.

The runner

An obnoxious group of big Bristol rugby players got loaded in a boozer and wobbled down to a Chinese restaurant just before closing. It was always their intention to be as offensive as possible to the diminutive waiters and then do a runner without paying when they'd had their fill.

So they insisted on sitting near to the door, ordered copious amounts of food and drink and set about singing racist songs and disrupting people on other tables. The waiters just served and ignored them. Until, that is, the rugby lads had finished their meal and asked for something that required the waiters to go behind the counter. Then the louts jumped up and all sprawled out on to the street to make their getaway. But the waiters were ready for them.

Within seconds an absolutely huge Chinese man-mountain in a string vest and bandana came charging out, brandishing a meat cleaver as big as his head, and chased the petrified lads. He grabbed them all at once and threw them on the pavement, crouched over the ringleader, grasped his throat and raised the cleaver, bringing it down with a crunch millimetres from the gibbering lad's forehead.

'Next time,' spat the grimacing Chinaman, 'I break your neck.'

The quivering nancies threw down all the money they had and scarpered pronto.

MYTHELLANEOUS

Food

★ The following are all aphrodisiacs: oysters, ground rhino horn, monkeys' genitalia, snakes' blood

★ American fizzy drinks make your stomach bleed

★ The Japanese are getting taller because they now eat hamburgers

★ Beef cattle's methane production is fuelling the greenhouse effect

★ The best Indian restaurants are where Indian people eat

★ Soufflés collapse if you slam a door

★ We don't get enough dirt in our diets

★ Late-night cheese sandwiches give you nightmares

★ We could go back to eating grass if we wanted to, because we've still got an appendix

MAN'S BEST FRIENDS

The animal kingdom at its least predictable

It's often said that ours is a nation of animal lovers, but here's a collection of hairy stories that suggest the feeling's not always mutual — and one story that implies some of us take the notion a bit too literally. This gaggle of cock and bull stories makes nonsense of horse-sense and proves that animals may be dumb, but they're not the only ones. We adore our creature comforts so much that when a comfort creature dies, it seems to strike a particular chord, and much more so than the passing of a fellow human. Mutts, moggies, budgies and porkers get their own back for our heavy-handed petting, in a series of animal anecdotes that certainly aren't tame . . .

The dead rabbit

My brother-in-law knows a cockney bloke who made his pile and moved his family out to the sticks, a really posh rustic village.

They weren't very popular in the new area because they were always banging car doors late at night, and they had one of those hyperactive dogs that's always yapping, chasing cyclists and catching things in nearby fields.

One day, though, the slavering hound came in with a rabbit between its teeth. Not just any rabbit, this was obviously a domestic bunny — and next-door's at that. The kid would be mortified at the fate of his cherished pet, and his mum was always going on about the tone of the neighbourhood going right down.

The cockney racked his brain for a solution. Luckily the dog hadn't chewed up the rabbit, only made it dirty by playing with it; it must have died of shock. He took the furry fatality and cleaned it up, shampooing and even carefully blow-drying it. Then he quickly checked no one was in next door, before hopping over the fence and nestling the rabbit back in the straw bedding of its hutch.

Later at the weekend, he was out in the garden drinking a can of lager, when he saw his next-door neighbour. This was the conversation he'd been dreading . . .

She said that little Jimmy was very, very upset. 'It's about the rabbit,' she said, as the bloke felt increasingly uncomfortable.

'I only buried it on Wednesday, but it was back in the hutch on Friday.'

The hungry Chihuahuas

A well-to-do spinster who lived in one of the better parts of Nuneaton hadn't been around for a few days, though she could normally be seen walking her three little Chihuahua dogs down the street to the park every day, always wrapped up in her best furs.

So a near neighbour went round to see if the old dear was okay; she was old and frail after all. When the neighbour reached the house, she saw what looked like two weeks' worth of milk in the doorway. Getting no reply, she called the police.

The boys in blue arrived and forced open the door to a nasty niff. When they came across the corpse, one of the officers fainted.

The old lady's famished Chihuahuas had nibbled away her face and extremities.

Sex with Nanny

According to a lawyer we know, in a court in North Wales in the 1970s, a woman was apparently suing her husband for divorce, on the grounds that the marriage had never been consummated. The only problem was, she was heavily pregnant at the time.

Smirking, the judge gently suggested her condition might have quite a large bearing on the case; either the marriage nuptials had taken place, or the woman had been unfaithful. The woman denied both. Sheepishly, she sincerely explained that she'd been having a sexual relationship with a ghost.

The judge kept a straight face and turned to the courtroom, asking if anyone else had ever had sex with a ghost. To his surprise, a ruddy-faced old farmer-type at the back looked around and timidly raised his hand.

Incredulous, the judge bellowed, 'You've really had sex with a ghost?'

'Oh,' said the old fellow, blanching, 'I thought you said "goat".'

Roach-prints

Two friends of mine lived in a squalid student flat in Hulme, Manchester, that was thoroughly infested with undesirable insects. Every night when they got in from the Union, they'd turn the hall light on, and hear an enormous clicking and scuttling sound across the lino in their kitchen. On their way through the kitchen to the toilet, they'd noticed that there was never any sign of an insect. Fast bastards!

Then one night they returned after a session, entered the hall and flicked the light switch, but the power had been cut off. So they both had to feel their way to the toilet in pitch blackness, alarmed by the strange crunching sound beneath each footstep they took. Then they went to bed.

In the morning they were sickened at the sight of their kitchen lino. Every spot where their feet had landed was marked out by shoe-shaped piles of crushed cockroaches.

The snappy crocodile

An adventurous friend of an old school pal went to northern Australia, to photograph the crocodiles. But even though his guide warned him several times against getting too close, he was recklessly determined to get a great shot.

More's the pity, for a huge mother croc with a scarred head sneaked up and lunged at him, tearing off his arm and swallowing it whole along with the expensive camera. In absolute agony, he was dragged away by his guide to a nearby hospital, where he was stitched and dosed up with painkillers.

But he was determined to have his limb sewn back on, and against everyone's advice checked himself out. Then, drugged up to the eyeballs, he drove painfully back to the scene of the attack with an experienced police croc-killer, and sought out the rotten reptile that did it.

When they tracked down the beast, the policeman shot it and slit it open. Quickly, they retrieved the man's arm, still holding the camera − but were shocked to find three other severed arms in the belly that hadn't even been reported missing.

The labrador let-off

A mate of my uncle's was working on his Ford Escort at the top of the hill in Ilford where he lived. In order to keep an eye on his Labrador dog, he'd locked it inside the car. He was working under the engine, when he heard a snarling sound, and then a mechanical clunk.

All of a sudden, the car rolled forwards, and he was just

able to scramble out of the way. He couldn't believe his eyes when he saw that his dog had taken the handbrake off and was standing with its paws on the steering wheel, as if it was driving. He was so surprised in fact that he didn't move fast enough to open the door, and the Escort careered halfway down the hill and ended up demolishing a neighbour's privet hedge.

[For more manic motoring, *see also* **Car Trouble**]

The scorpion 'down under'

A middle-aged couple from Norfolk went to Australia to stay with relatives and, being big fans of nature programmes, planned to go walkabout in the bush. So they stayed in a rudimentary shack in the outback.

The first night they were there, they stayed up late thinking about the fabulous time they were going to have. When they eventually got into their rough single bed, they lay on their backs for some time excitedly listening to the sounds of the wild. Then, for the first time in a while, they made love.

In the morning, they woke up cramped next to each other. The husband sprang out of bed and opened the curtains. Then, as he returned to bed, he shouted to his wife to jump up.

There, twitching on the sheet, was a lethal scorpion. It had been there all night. Fortunately, it was upside down, and, as we all know, scorpions can only sting when they're upright.

Parrot fashion

A friend of my mum's knew a woman whose husband bought a prattling parrot that his wife grew to despise utterly. The bird seemed to sense this somehow, but never pecked her or anything.

But what annoyed this woman more than the parrot was how suddenly whenever she sat down to watch a programme she liked, the TV switched to another channel and she had to flash it back using the remote. Then it would switch again. This palaver went on for weeks, and especially when the *Neighbours* theme tune came on.

Then one day a friend was round with her dog. When *Neighbours* came on screen, the channel changed again, and the dog jumped up, howling at the parrot. The channel was switched back again, and the same thing happened.

It transpired that the parrot had apparently learned how to mimic the supersonic tones emitted by the remote, and was using his skill to wind up his adversary, the poor wife.

> Of course, everyone knows that channel-flashers don't use ultrasound to send their signals; it's radiation really.

Paws for thought

An English family were sightseeing in the famous American nature reserve Yellowstone Park in a hired station wagon, and stopped abruptly when they found themselves surrounded by a posse of large bears.

After a while they determined to proceed slowly through them, making sure windows were wound up. As they moved off, they found one bear was following them close behind and howling aggressively. They sped up a little, but the howling bear just trotted faster, keeping right behind them.

Eventually, the car was travelling so speedily that the exhausted bear fell over and lay down in the road growling in a high-pitched fashion. When they arrived back at their hotel, they went to the trunk to remove their picnic things and noticed, to their eternal shame, a patch of bloody fur and two of the unfortunate bear's claws, jammed behind the wagon's sharp chrome bumper.

> Any resemblance between this and The Edinburgh skinheads [*see* **Urban Classics**] is purely deliberate and should be seen solely as a ploy to take up space.

Monkey-hanging business

A classic English myth concerns the people of Hartlepool on the north-east coast, an allegedly simple folk and even simpler in the time of the story, which took place during the Napoleonic wars at the beginning of the nineteenth century.

Apparently, a fleet of French ships was sighted in the North Sea and harried by English vessels until they were virtually obliterated. But one of Boney's boats was seen sailing just off the coast of Hartlepool, and local braves were sent out to apprehend it for king and country.

This they did with little difficulty, for the crew was entirely absent save for a little monkey dressed in a tiny uniform of Napoleon's navy. Never having seen a Frenchman before, and with no one to compare him with, the good populace of Hartlepool arrested him as an enemy sailor. The monkey was then tried, pronounced guilty and hanged. And with no character witnesses . . .

This story is still the source of some discomfort to Hartlepudlians. Mindful of the potential for mischief, local lads from neighbouring towns (Sunderland, Newcastle, Middlesbrough) occasionally dress up in monkey costumes and go on pub crawls around Hartlepool — to be followed around by bad-tempered youths with a score to settle.

Another angle lies in the spread of this myth. There are Kent people who swear the monkey-hanging townsfolk were natives of their county — all other details remaining the same. If you know of any other places that should be twinned with Hartlepool for their animal activities, the authors would love to hear about them.

For the record, there's a theme pub on Cleveland Street, London W1, that displays the whole sorry story.

Billy the Seal

In the thirties, Cardiff had a little zoological area in Victoria Park where a monkey, some deer, and a seal called Billy resided. One week it rained heavily for days, and the town was flooded. The deluge was so bad that the park was under-water, and Billy the Seal made his escape.

The authorities found him very elusive, though sightings were numerous – one witness even claimed to have seen him boarding a tram. Eventually, though, hunger was the undoing of Billy the Seal. The slippery customer was finally caught after two week's liberty, trying to swipe fish from a fishmongers.

The purring engine

There's a persistent story that a student driving back down to London from York at the end of his course packed all his gear, checked his car over, then went out for a final night's drinking. In the morning, he rose early, got straight into his car and drove all the way down south without stopping.

When he arrived at his parents' house, he got out and began unpacking, but could hear a feeble whining sound. He worked out it was coming from under the bonnet, and when he opened it, found his flatmate's blackened, frightened kitten perched on top of the air filter.

'Hangdog' Hannah

Some relatives of a friend's friend live in rural Ireland, very isolated from the ways of the modern world. They're an extended family headed by a fearsome matriarch pleasantly called 'Hangdog' Hannah, due to her practice of not neutering her dogs and mercilessly dispatching the resultant puppies.

Hannah also has four beefy boys. On one occasion the lads got back to the cottage after one of their regular late-night drinking sessions, and set about making a cup of tea. The cottage wasn't on mains supply, so one of the lads took a big kettle and fished water out of the rainwater tub outside. They drank the tea and all agreed there was nothing like a cup of tea made with God's own water. But this cup had been particularly nice.

So one of the boys set about making another pot. To his horror, though, when he poured the old water out of the kettle, a newly drowned puppy flopped out. Hannah had been up to her old canine-culling tricks again.

Granma's toes

The same rural Irish family had a huge bony hound which they rarely fed, and an ageing Granny, immobilised by arthritis from the hips down. One Saturday night, as was their habit, 'Hangdog' Hannah and her boys went out for a heavy drinking session, leaving Granny asleep in front of the fire, and their wolfhound there to guard her.

When they returned much later, they crept in so as not to wake Granny, who was still snoring feebly in front of the embers. However, they could see their hound tugging at her feet.

When they shooed it away, they saw that Granny's unfeeling feet had been liberated of three of their toes.

Two typical urbanite impressions of the incivil-
ity of rural life. And all true. . .

Uncool for cats

My uncle used to be a long distance lorry driver, and a mate of his on the Manchester to Glasgow run had a rather nasty experience.

One cold winter's night the rain was bucketing down, and the lorry driver had his headlights and wipers full on just to be able to see enough to carry on. He'd had a flat tyre earlier in the day and was driving on late through the atrocious conditions in a vain attempt to make up time. Peering out of the steamed-up windscreen, white knuckles clutching the steering wheel, his headlights suddenly picked out a startled cat frozen with fear in the middle of the road.

He slammed on the anchors, the lorry skidded, and there was a horrible bump.

Now the lorry driver was a cat lover himself, and feeling sickeningly guilty, leapt from his cab to find the stricken animal. It was writhing in agony on the roadside verge, so he did the decent thing: took out his shovel and put it out of its misery.

After that nasty turn, the driver continued on his way but pulled over at the next pub to steady his nerves. He'd just begun to calm down with a half of bitter, when a policeman entered the inn and arrested him. A tearful old lady had just rung them.

It appears she'd popped out to call her beloved moggy in from the appalling weather and had seen the lorry run over next-door's cat. Her own feline had been playing around in some long grass by the side of the road, when the lorry driver had pulled up, got out and despatched it with his spade.

For some reason, felines incur our wrath more than their canine rivals. This next story is often attributed to Reginald Bosanquet. Whether he read it out on *News at Ten*, or used to tell it at his many after-dinner speaking engagements, we're not quite sure. But there do seem to be a number of different versions. Here's one we were told recently:

'Green Goddess' cat

During the firemen's strike in the early eighties, the Government brought in the army to fight fires in a bid not to deal with the firemen's pay claim. Although public support was largely behind the firemen, the squaddies using the famous 'Green Goddess' fire engines, stirred popular nostalgia. The soldiers became heroes and the Green Goddesses became the stuff of urban legends.

It was during this time that a Green Goddess was called out to attend a dire emergency, the fireman's worst nightmare: a cat up a tree. The fire engine arrived at the scene of the tragedy to the cheers of a huge crowd. The soldiers trooped out, raised the ladder and positioned it against the tree.

A young private scrambled nimbly up, along the branch, rescued the stranded puss and was straight down the ladder lickety-split.

The crowd roared its approval and the squaddies were slapped on the back and applauded. The cat belonged to an old lady who rushed out with cups of tea in gratitude to the soldiers. Eventually the squaddies got back into their Green Goddess, waved to the jubliant crowed, revved up the trusty old engine and ran over the same cat, who'd inadvisedly fallen asleep under the big back wheels.

The S-bend snake

Ever since they struck oil in the Middle East, it's been said that rich Arabs have been buying up the posher parts of London. One particular family owned a large apartment in the swankiest bit of Kensington. I think they might even have been royal or something.

Anyway they were rolling in it — gold-plated Rolls-Royce, the lot. They had a number of live-in servants who had their own quarters. It's often the case that those with the ackers have short arms and long pockets, and this family were no exception.

They paid peanuts and most of their staff were foreign nationals not keen to kick up a fuss about pay and conditions. The maid was Portuguese and didn't speak a word of English, or, for that matter, Arabic.

One day when she was cleaning, she came running out of the toilet screaming her head off. Her employers couldn't understand what she was gibbering about, so they went to investigate but couldn't find anything.

This began to happen again and again, the maid would run out of the bathroom screaming and although she tried to explain in sign language what had terrified her, they just thought she was round the bend.

It wasn't until they heard reports of their upstairs

neighbour's missing exotic pet that all became clear. The escaped gargantuan anaconda had been hiding out in the flat's water system, haunting the S-bend and rearing up whenever the terrified maid had tried to scrub the pan.

> In Miami, where the problem of escaped pets has reached epidemic proportions, the authorities employ a bloke to track down all the snakes, crocs, tigers and monitor lizards abandoned or flushed away by their owners when they get too big, and which grow even bigger on the rich pickings of Florida's waste. This risky job was the subject of a recent BBC TV documentary.

The cannibal wolfhound

This one was told in all seriousness by a well-regarded local rag-maker, a regular of the Brown Cow on the top side of Bury, Lancs.

He was taking his Irish wolfhound 'Arfa' (half a Guinness) for a walk up on the moors just near where he lives. It was a lovely sunny day, they'd been up the top, round the reservoir, he'd smoked a pipe and they were on their way back down. The dog had run ahead as usual.

When he caught up with the wolfhound, it was shaking its head violently. Thinking the dog had caught a rat, he took it by the scruff of the neck and said 'Drop it, drop it, boy.' The dog did as bid, but to his horror it wasn't a rat, it was the Yorkshire terrier from next door, quite dead.

That story is a variation on one of the all-time classic, the 'Choking Doberman'. [*See* The fingered felon, **Urban Classics**.]

Trunk and disorderly

Our kid's schoolmate's dad used to drink in The Hare and Hounds, a pub up on the north side of Manchester. He was in there every night putting away the pints, from just after opening time right up to last orders and, despite his wife's protestations, he always took the car.

One day the circus came to town, and as usual they pitched their tent just up from the top road which led to The Hare and Hounds. It was raining as usual and quite misty when by chance two of the elephants escaped from the big top, and were soon lost in the murky gloom. Our kid's mate's dad was in the pub having a rare old time, and missed all the radio broadcasts about the missing pachyderms.

By chucking-out time he'd had a real skinful. He staggered out to the car park, got in his Zephyr, put on his James Last cassette and hit the road. The fog was a real pea-souper; you couldn't see your hand in front of your face. He was driving really slowly, weaving along, when his full-beam headlights picked out two huge grey swaying shapes in the middle of the road. The police found the car the next day, doors open, lights full on and keys still in the ignition. The old man hasn't driven or touched a drop since.

Circuses, with their travelling assortment of performers and exotic animals, lend themselves perfectly to Urban Mythology, and crop up with some regularity. The story above deviates from the other strangely ubiquitous 'escaped elephant' tale, in which one of the heavy beasts sits on the boot or bonnet of a car, denting it badly.

Not too trilled

Some friends were staying with their elderly grandmother in her rose-covered cottage down in Dorset. Granny had popped out to a Women's Institute meeting and the young couple were left in charge of the cottage, and more importantly her budgie.

Granny's cherished companion was hopping around twittering and pecking his cuttlefish in a frustrated fashion, so they thought they'd be kind and let the bird out to stretch its wings. After diligently checking that the doors and windows were shut fast and the cat was out of the room, they opened the door to his little cage.

The budgie burst out and flew hell-for-leather around the room, it got so over-excited at its new-found freedom that sadly it crash-landed and broke its leg.

The couple were mortified — what would Granma say? So they gently scooped up the feathered casualty and attempted to administer some first aid. The poor little chap was writhing in agony, so they made a tiny splint out of a matchstick and fastened it to the broken limb with cotton.

They were just tidying up the makeshift support when disaster struck. As he moved to cut the end of the cotton, the grandson accidentally snipped off the budgie's other leg.

Yucky Yucca

A work colleague told me about her friend who had a nasty experience with an exotic parlour palm. She'd been out shopping in everyone's mum's favourite store, famous for its reliability and underwear, and purchased a Yucca plant. It was a fine specimen and immediately it took pride of place in the living-room, and was looked after with extra special care.

It was while watering the parlour palm that she noticed an ominous clicking noise coming from the plant. At first she thought nothing of it, but it nagged away at her and at each watering the sound seemed to get worse. So she called up the store to complain.

The person who answered the phone was most anxious. She told the woman to stay exactly where she was, not to touch the plant or go near it, and said there would be someone straight round.

A few minutes later there was a knock on the door and four men in head-to-toe protective clothing, looking like something out of *Aliens*, came into the living-room and spread out a large rubber sheet. They put the Yucca in the middle of the sheet and carefully lifted it out of its pot . . . to reveal a large mother tarantula with hundreds of babies crouched in the black fur of her back.

That's another hardy perennial tabloid-style myth. In fact, in April 1992 (not the 1st!), a London radio news broadcast resurrected the old chestnut of a trader at Spitalfields market being bitten by a spider that came out of a bunch of bananas shipped in from Colombia. As usual, though, there was no name, no interview . . . no proof.

It's a well-known fact that the north is packed out with folk in baggy trousers, braces and ratting caps, eating black puddings, carrying baskets of championship racing pigeons around and swilling pints of bitter — and that's just the women . . . Here's a brace of bird stories to tickle any true pigeon lover's fancy:

Coming a cropper

A young lad my mum knows moved from a picturesque Yorkshire village to a chip shop near Belle Vue Aces Speedway track in Ardwick, Manchester and he was missing his friends.

His dad, well aware of his son's predicament, returned home from the pub one night with a curious basket. Inside the lad was thrilled to find a stunning racing pigeon with distinctive red markings. It was a real beauty.

Dad, who was a joiner by trade, quickly knocked up a pigeon loft on top of the shed where they cut the spuds into chips, with a special wire-netting part so the bird could see out and get used to its new surroundings.

A few weeks later the young pigeon fancier had got to know a few of the local scallywags, and after several soapings of its wings and lots of encouragement, his bird was ready for its first flight.

The lad took his prize possession down the Red Rec playing fields where some of his new mates were having a game of footy. They all gasped when they saw the fabulous bird. Proudly the lad held it aloft and give it a gentle send-off. The bird flew round impressing the crowd with its grace and agility, but suddenly there was a sharp crack and the bird fell to the ground. Rushing to the pigeon's rescue, the lads were horrified to find a pellet hole in its chest. The yobbos from the next street had shot it with an air rifle.

Back at home the lad tried to nurse his pride and joy back to health. But every time he fed it corn, the stuff dropped out of the pellet hole. Unless he thought of something quick the bird would die of starvation.

It was when he was rooting through the kitchen that he came across the first aid kit and the solution.

From then on the red beauty could often be seen flying the skies of deepest Ardwick, sporting an Elastoplast on its crop.

Home sweet homer

The same lad apparently decided to buy a feathered friend for his red pigeon and set off on the bus clutching his five shillings (a lot of money in the fifties) down to Withy Grove Market. The pigeon sellers were next to the second-hand book stalls, and he soon set his heart on a blue-grey bird with white feathers in its wings, and coughed up the five bob.

Every pigeon fancier knows that you put soap on a bird's wings to stop it flying off, so it gets used to the new loft and the view over the rooftops and recognises them as home.

The bird was well fed on the best corn, and eventually as the soap flaked off its wings it launched itself for its maiden flight. The pigeon circled once or twice, then gaining confidence headed off towards the city centre — and never came back.

On his next visit to the market the lad looked carefully in the bird boxes. He felt sure he'd seen one bird before, but who would believe a lad of his age?

Anti-climax

Some time back, a Mexican city near Guadalajara faced the dire threat of a huge river of ants which were heading directly for it, some miles away. These weren't just any ants, oh no, these were voracious soldier ants that destroy everything in their path, and of a size you only seem to get in Latin America.

The city authorities were warned about the danger and set about trying to stop the relentless column of oversize arthropods, and tried all sorts of measures: machine-gunned them, bombed them, dug trenches in their path, poured boiling oil on them, set up booby traps.

But the columns of ravenous ants couldn't be diverted from their course, and a civic disaster appeared unavoidable.

Then one of the burghers had a brain-wave, and the city gave it a go as a last gasp effort. They built a huge picnic just north of the city.

It worked. The rapacious insects swerved off from their course and headed for the slap-up decoy, and the city was miraculously saved.

Bacon lined

My grandad told me that when he was a lad, he and his mates used to play a cunning trick on the feathered residents of a large pond near where they lived in Droylsden, Manchester.

The lads would go up to the pond, take a length of string and tie a piece of fatty bacon rind to it. The hungry, unsuspecting ducks would swim over thinking they were in for a treat. The lads would throw the bacon rind to the first duck who'd snaffle it up immediately.

Now it's a little known fact that bacon rind goes through a duck much like string through a goose (makes sense) – or even a dose of salts, whichever is the quickest. Anyway, the rind passed straight through the duck and floated on the water, the next starving duck gobbled it up. The same thing happened again and again until there was a long line of ducks all connected by a piece of string.

The lads would lead them around for a while, then take one duck and start pulling its leg just like I'm pulling yours.

> We're not totally sure about biological accuracy relating to the speed of a duck's digestive system, or whether one duck would fancy eating something which had so recently passed through another duck. All we can say is please don't try this at home.

Dirty dog

A politician at the last general election was canvassing his large constituency and came to a terraced house with a slavering pit bull outside. He hated dogs, and was a bit hesitant as he pressed the doorbell, but he was given a warm welcome by the people of the house.

They told him they always voted for him anyway, and pleased to meet him, invited him in for a cup of tea. He was feeling pretty parched after a tough morning's door-stepping and accepted their offer, edging past the growling pit bull.

The dog followed him to heel into the room and lay down showing its teeth and staring at him from the middle of the floor.

He was enjoying his cup of tea as much as he could with the dog there, chatting with his constituents about local issues, when the dog stood up, cocked its leg and completely soaked the carpet. His hosts looked at the dog briefly, then carried on talking.

The politician was a bit taken aback, but as no one else said anything, he just wondered a bit about what kind of supporter he was attracting. Each to their own, he decided.

After a good chinwag, the candidate drained his cup, thanked the family, and made his way out of the door. He'd just taken a few paces outside when he heard someone call out behind him:

'Excuse me, aren't you going to take your dog with you?'

Posing pouch

The crew from a British magazine were going on a fashion shoot in the Australian outback, and were driving along an empty dirt road in their Shogun 4×4, when from nowhere a kangaroo suddenly bounded into their path, and they hit it full on.

They all jumped out to see if it was okay, but it had quite obviously died of shock. The tasteless art director of the shoot decided it would be a great gimmick to make use of the poor creature and lobbed the carcass in the boot.

Then, when they arrived at their location, he dressed the kangaroo up in some of the expensive designer clobber the models were supposed to wear, and propped it up to take the snaps.

But in the blink of a shutter, the kangaroo recovered from its concussion, stood up and bounded off into the bush, still wearing the glamorous creations of Jean-Paul Gaultier, Yoji Yamomoto and Mr Byrite.

Having a truffle '

A woman and her boyfriend went on holiday to Germany. But the campsite they had booked up to stay at was right next to a noisy farm occupied by aggressive-sounding pigs, and smelt bloody awful.

To make matters worse, there were no proper toilets. If you wanted to do number twos, the only available area was the woods, where the huge, ever-hungry pigs sometimes rooted and snorted around.

The second night of their stay, the man was overtaken with the desire to pass a motion, and he succumbed to it. Carefully negotiating the barbed wire divide, he dropped his trousers and squatted uncomfortably in the pigs' wood, keeping a watchful eye out for marauding hogs in the darkness.

Within minutes, while he was still at his labours, he was violently nudged off his feet from behind by a scoffing sow, ravenous for some fresh food.

> Of course, they do things differently abroad [*see also* Private viewing, **Travel Sickness**]. British toilet training and its psychological legacy has led to an odd assortment of blimpish myths about trying to pass a motion abroad, including one about Thailand, where it's rumoured that you have to defecate through hatches in the floors of houses on stilts (the houses, not you). Sometimes, the hungry pigs wallowing in the mud beneath get over-enthusiastic and snatch your waste by shoving their heads through the hole soon after you've got into position.

The dead budgie

A friend's gran called in some plumbers to fix a dodgy old gas fire in her house in Aberdeen. The blokes turned up on the allotted day and set to fixing the fire. Gran decided to pop out down the shops while they were on the job, and did so.

The gas-fitters were a right couple of cowboys. They kept on dropping the monkey wrench and smashing tiles on the fireplace, and there were bits of the fire all over the shop. What's more, the gas fire was leaking like a sieve while they were messing about. Eventually, though, they got it back together with only a few nuts and washers left over at the end.

As they stood up to have a fag, one of them noticed that the budgie had fallen off its perch and was lying on the floor of its cage with its little legs in the air — stone dead. Realising there'd be hell to pay when the old lady came home and saw they'd gassed her pet, the two bodgers took some copper wire and fastened the deceased bird upright on his perch. Then they cleared up, and were ready to be off when they heard the keys in the door.

The old lady came into the living-room, took one look at the budgie's cage and fainted.

When they'd revived her, she explained that she had been deeply shocked to see the budgie on its perch again — as it had died earlier that morning.

[*See also* The carpet creeper, **Occupational Hazards**]

MYTHELLANEOUS

Animals

★ The only racing certainty is a horse with a hot spud shoved up its arse. That horse will win

★ How to avoid shark bites: dodge out of the way when its eyes close at the last minute; see it off with a punch to its nose

★ There's a massive snake at large in a lake in Siberia with the head of a sheep

★ Piranhas can strip a horse to the bone in three seconds

★ The new breed of London rodent, the super-rat, is immune to any poison known to man

★ If you hold a dog's bottom jaw, it can't bite you

★ Llamas can spit in your eye at thirty paces

★ Parrots find swear words easier to learn than any others

★ Kittens can go through a whole washing-machine cycle and only feel a little dizzy

★ Bats generally get tangled in your hair

OCCUPATIONAL HAZARDS

Weird tales from the workplace

The workplace is a most fertile ground for myth production, and this little lot prove that most accidents don't happen in the home. Perhaps it's the fierceness of internal office politics, perhaps the nine-to-five tedium, or perhaps just the liquid lunches, that makes minds wander into the realms of vindictive fantasy. Health and safety take second place when there's a job to be done, especially an 'odd' one. The spirit of 'the long stand' lives on . . .

The deer-stalker

A friend of mine recalls a man at his office who was quite high-up but a pompous old buffer, and therefore unpopular with his workmates. One day, he was browsing in the local market and came across a Sherlock Holmes-style deer-stalker hat, which he bought and wore to work, to everyone's quiet amusement.

Unfortunately for him, a few days later, two of his colleagues chanced upon the same market stall, and decided to purchase two more identical titfers − one in the largest size available, the other the smallest.

The next day, he hung his 'stalker up in reception as usual. The two colleagues whipped it off its hook, replacing it with the large one they'd bought. At the end of the day, the old buffer picked up the hat and put it on, and was quite surprised to find that it was far too big, but he didn't think much about it and went home with the hat resting on his ears.

The next day, they replaced the largest hat with the smallest, which perched precariously on top of his cranium . . . and so they went on, day after day for weeks − sometimes leaving the bloke's original hat for a few days − until eventually the distraught old buffer paid a visit to his GP, convinced that his head was expanding and contracting like a balloon.

Blackout

A friend who works in the West End of London, around Soho, reckons the area is plagued with road works. Rogue gangs of cowboys and sub-contractors are forever tearing the place apart, and often seem to have little idea of what they're doing or what they might hit. They just seem to pitch up in a knackered transit, throw out a few cones and start drilling. The noise round there is appalling.

Anyway, this mate was flicking through his Filofax one day when there was a huge bang and a blinding flash in the street outside, and all the power in the office went off. He looked outside to see a man clambering out at the edge of the hole he had been digging, still clutching his pneumatic drill. The weird thing was he was charred black and giving off plumes of smoke. He'd found an electricity cable.

The workman stayed rooted to the spot until the ambulance arrived to take him away.

Lift logger

In Los Angeles in the mid-seventies, there was a spate of strange crimes in two of the city's busiest and biggest office blocks — you know, those ninety-storey mirror-glass sky-scrapers.

This involved a mystery assailant crapping into the lifts when they were empty, only for someone to walk into the elevator to discover the neat stool soon after. This happened two or three days a week.

The mystery deepened when after hundreds of complaints the office security guards were put in charge of the problem.

Despite almost constant surveillance and the bolting down of all hatches, etc., the phantom crapper still managed to perpetrate his regular dirty deed — sometimes with the elevator empty for barely a minute.

Entirely undetected for three months, the lift logger stopped as suddenly as he'd begun. Security never got to the bottom of it.

Papier man-mâché

A friend who worked as a safety officer in a large Lancashire paper mill knew of a workmate who put himself about a bit. The mill took all sorts of paper waste — newspapers, cardboard packaging — and pulped it in massive vats with huge revolving blades at the bottom for recycling.

Every now and then, a load of girlie mags would arrive for pulping, though many would disappear before reaching the threshing blades. One day, just such a porn consignment arrived.

Now the vats were about sixty feet deep, but when they were full, you could reach the top of the mush. Anyway, this fellow was a bit of a lech and as he watched the mags circulating, he was overtaken by furtive urges and tried to fish out a top-shelfer.

But being a stumpy bloke he couldn't quite reach. So he made sure no one was near, moved the safety mesh away and got a chair to lean further over. However, in his frustrated frenzy he must have lost his balance and toppled into the vat, because around an hour later safety officers found just the chair and the open mesh.

There was no chance of him surviving, so the managers decided not to shut down the process, and the mill continued happily churning out cornflake packets.

Another widespread myth, that one. Two nice variations have come to our attention, both, strangely, set in the north-west of England. The first one gives the location as a brewery. The story goes that when the bloke falls in the boiling vat, the factory boss decides it won't affect the flavour of the bitter, and the process continues. (Obviously made up by someone from t'other side of t'Pennines.) The second, and our favourite, has a bloke working in an animal processing plant on the Fylde coast, who is rendered useless by the larding procedure. Again, the line manager decides no one will notice a bit of human in there, and allows the process to continue. The effect on sales isn't recorded.

Green side up

Some years back a couple who run our local pub went to see about buying a new Barratt home. The estate was still being built, so the foreman took them on a tour of the show house.

But as he showed them round the living-room, he looked through the window and shouted out 'Green side up!' without a word to the couple. The same thing happened again on the first floor: looked out the window, 'Green side up!'

When it happened a third time, the two could hardly stop themselves laughing, though still they didn't know what he was on about. Eventually they asked him why he kept going on about 'green side up', and he explained.

'It's this hopeless lot,' he moaned, pointing to his site workers. 'You can't even leave them alone to lay the lawns.'

'Who's a naughty boy, then?'

My mate Billy is a fireman, and he's full of horror stories about death on the London tubes, because it's the fire service that has to clean up all the suicides who throw themselves under trains. Understandably a certain type of gallows humour has developed.

One time, he was cleaning up a suicide on the Northern Line, putting various bits of body scattered over a mile of track into bags, but when they re-assembled the body in an ambulance, they found they were missing an arm. This meant a trek right down the tunnel again, so they were pretty narked.

Down they trooped, and half an hour later, one of the officers emerged into the light with the arm tucked vertically out of the front of his jacket, slapping the hand against his face and saying in a Mr Punch voice, 'Who's a naughty boy, then? Who's a naughty boy, then?'

Apparently, the favourite London stations to pop your clogs are leafy ones on the Jubilee and Central lines. Just in case you were wondering.

Baptism of fire

The same fireman friend had a baptism of fire — almost literally — when he first joined the force as a green twenty-one year old. On his first day's active duty, he turned up at the station to find it throbbing with loud music, and full of half-dressed women being chased around by firemen that were very much the worse for drink.

Shocked at what he saw, the rookie turned down all the cans offered him, and found a quiet room where he could keep a clear head in case of emergencies.

A few hours into his shift, with the station party still all systems go, the alarm sounded, and the crew were alerted to a big factory fire some miles away.

But there was a big problem: one of the usual drivers was far too inebriated to drive legally, and the other was asleep in a drunken stupor. The lads turned to the rookie as the only sober person left. He admitted he held a drivers' licence, but nothing like the qualification needed for driving one of the huge red fire engines.

However, with his colleagues imploring him and duty calling, he submitted to pressure and gingerly drove the vehicle on a hairy white-knuckle journey to the fire. They eventually arrived forty-five minutes late, with other crews already there and local TV cameras rolling.

The drunken, motley fire crew set about tackling the blaze, but cameras turned away from them two minutes later when the rest of the still inebriated posse made a dramatic entry: three of them in full uniform hanging out of a beaten-up old Escort, two of them perched precariously on a swerving moped, with fire hats instead of crash helmets; and all captured for posterity by the grateful TV company.

The unlucky ladders

A friend of mine used to have a Saturday job, sweeping up in a big warehouse in Cheetham Hill. The warehouse was a huge jerry-built monstrosity, and bits of it were always falling down or crumbling away. Keeping it in good order was like painting the Forth Bridge – a never-ending challenge.

One cold autumn day, the maintenance man was up some very high ladders painting the mainframe. The ladders went right up to the roof, and the bloke was seeing to a corroded cross-member when the piece he was steadying himself on tumbled away and he fell all of fifty feet to the concrete floor below.

Strangely, he landed on his feet, but the force of the drop drove his legs up into his body and through his shoulders. He tottered around silently in very small circles before keeling over stone dead.

The carpet creeper

Some friends of our family bought a new carpet in the January sales and took full advantage of the offer of a free fitting.

The following week, two scruffy herberts purporting to be carpet fitters arrived in a filthy van to perform the task. Surprisingly, the pair did a fair job of laying the floor covering, and when they'd finished they stood back to have a fag and admire their own handiwork. One of them noticed a small lump right in the middle of the carpet and pointed it out to his partner, who quickly reached for the hammer and with some carefully aimed blows flattened out the bump. Shortly afterwards, the mother of the household came in to thank them, but with a troubled demeanour. 'You've done a lovely job on the carpet . . . but I don't suppose you've seen our hamster hiding anywhere have you?'

> The best known variation of this story involves the ubiquitous cowboy workmen and a budgie under the wallpaper, an idea used recently in a radio ad performed by Michael Bentine. Another adland urban myth is the Skol commercial, where a new boyfriend throws a ball for the dog in a high-rise flat. The ball takes an unlucky bounce and flies out of the window with the dog diving after it.

The hand bag

A mate of mine is a bus driver in Newcastle. He and his workmates find all sorts of things abandoned on their buses.

Once he found a brown paper bag on a seat when he got to the terminus. He opened it and found a human hand inside. It still hasn't been claimed.

> Makes a change from umbrellas.

Tube runner

A mate who works on the London Underground claims he knows about a particularly bizarre incident that happened on the Northern Line.

The train was rattling along briskly when passengers in the first carriage felt the emergency brake go on, and they were treated to the rare sight of the driver's door bursting open and the driver himself running hell-for-leather back through the carriages and connecting doors with a manic expression on his face.

The unmanned train screeched to a halt — as it turned out just inches from another tube train that had broken down in the tunnel.

There are quite a few strange stories associated with the London Underground. Apparently the London tube system runs on computer software designed in Delhi — not as bad as you might think, as their railway is the most efficient in the world, so they say. Another little known 'fact' relates to the 'mind the gap' message which booms out at Bank station every time a train arrives. The voice is that of the tannoy system salesman who only did the recording as a test to sell the equipment, back in the seventies. Not only have London Underground used it ever since, apparently they've never paid out a penny in royalties.

Plumbing new depths

An electrician was on site putting the finishing touches to a brand new detached house on a prestigious new estate. He was connecting the electricity upstairs to start with, working his way down, while the other craftsmen were labouring downstairs.

All morning his gurgling stomach had been playing up after last night's suicidally hot phal curry, so he nipped downstairs at lunchtime to find the toilet and let it all hang out.

All the other geezers were out to lunch − literally − and so the sparkie made his way to the lavvy, took the *Daily Mirror* out of his back pocket and settled down for a lengthy clearance.

Twenty minutes later, he'd finished riding the porcelain Honda, bib and braces round his ankles, and set about doing the paperwork.

Then he stood up to flush the chain − but there wasn't a chain, or a cistern, or a waste pipe for that matter. In fact, the toilet hadn't even been plumbed in yet . . .

Log roll

When the Tiger Bay docks in Cardiff were proper working ones and not just a yuppie playground, they used to have huge, deep rectangular pools of water there chock-full of thick, long tree trunks, in storage before being sawn up or shipped overseas.

The pools weren't very secure, and kids often used to sneak down to them in the evening or at weekends to play, despite warnings about the mortal perils lurking on site. The biggest dare was to try and run from one side of the pool to the other, fifty feet across the treacherous floating logs.

None of the local kids had the bottle to give it a go, but one winter's day a plucky little adolescent put it about that he was going to attempt the log run that evening. After the last worker had left the docks, a crowd of youngsters gathered around the pool to watch the spectacle.

The lad arrived looking determined, and, with his mates egging him on, took off his jacket and prepared to run.

He set off at a fierce pace, and easily skipped across the slippery trunks until he got right in the middle. Then he jumped a little gap that had suddenly appeared, and lost his footing as he landed.

The children all gasped as they saw him slip into the freezing water between the heavy logs, which immediately closed up around him in the pool. Too terrified for their own safety to run across to save him, the kids watched horrified as the plucky lad made desperate efforts to clamber back on to a tree trunk.

But when his hand reached out of the water, the log rolled and he was thrown back down into the icy water. Time after time the same thing happened.

But still the children prayed he'd make it, until finally his exhausted little hand reached out no more, and the log pool went a deathly calm.

Incoming tax

Some of us are born to genius, others only aspire to being

filthy rich. The bloke in this story combined both.

A young postie in Shipley, Bradford, found the job didn't live up to his expectations, and while on his rounds hatched a money-making scheme to set him up for a life of luxurious leisure.

His plan was dead simple. On his patch was a big Inland Revenue office, to which people from all over the country sent off as little money as they could get away with. The plotting postie lived in a quiet village and picked a particularly parochial building society to open up a new account.

Although his friends were impressed by the postie's new-found wealth, they couldn't work out where he'd got the moolah from, and he wouldn't let on. But his Bunsen-burner from the Royal Mail was meagre, and he didn't have any sidelines where he could earn a few extra bob. After a few months, their questions were answered when a warrant went out for his arrest.

Apparently, he'd been intercepting the mail to the tax office on his round and paying it into his building society account . . . opened under the name 'I. Revenue'.

> Variations on this popular theme include the postie making deposits under the name 'Inlandia Revenue', or only being caught when he arrives in the works car park driving a brand new bright red Porsche. Another notorious example relates to a temporary employee of the Independent Producers Association (IPA) whose goose was almost cooked when the company toilet overflowed after thousands of empty envelopes were stuffed down the bowl.

The crafty culprit slipped clean away, along with the contents of his building society account in the name of 'Mr Ipa'.

MYTHELLANEOUS

Occupations

★ The Royal Family work really hard: 'The Queen? I wouldn't do her job for love nor money'

★ London taxi-drivers are scared to cross water

★ Catholic priests never have children

★ All teachers like apples

★ All butchers' dogs are fit

★ All air stewardesses are in the 'mile high club'

★ All people who work in chocolate factories never touch the stuff

★ All biscuit factory workers habitually spit on the product

★ All vicars always want more tea and cake

★ All footballers' haircuts are done by the same barber

★ All barbers are bald

★ All dentists have bad breath

★ All park-keepers are grumpy

MILITARY MYTHS

Over the top escapades

When you take the king's shilling, you invest in a world of khaki catastrophes and a weird set of beliefs untouched by the strict discipline and solid professionalism of the services or the march of time. There's a uniform conviction that when you bite the bullet, if the enemy doesn't get you the food probably will. We're talking Sod's Law, martial lore, here — lots of death, but bugger all glory. That's what happens when too many men spend too long in their own company.

It's often remarked that at the time of the Great War, during lulls in the slaughter either (or both) sides in the conflict would chuck down their weapons at the drop of a (tin) hat and kick a ball around. A friend's grandad used to tell a story of one such episode involving his father's platoon in France.

On a sunny day when there'd been no bombardment for nearly a week, the bored Tommies set up a huge soccer game on the edge of No Man's Land, playing in full uniform in case of attack.

The game lasted until early evening when a wayward shot lofted the ball way out into the craters of the blasted no-go zone. By coincidence, a heavy German bombardment began at the same time, and the lads ducked down back into their trenches. Some of them, despite the slight distraction of flying bullets, shells and the like, scanned No Man's Land for the lost ball — it was their only one. Eventually, Great Grandad saw it, and the platoon resolved to retrieve it under cover of darkness, one of them keeping an unblinking eye on the ball so as not to lose track of it.

As the guns grew silent and light faded away, Great Grandad, as he put it, drew the short straw to slip out and dodge the snipers' fire and repatriate the football. So he crossed himself, jumped over the top and zig-zagged his way through the pitch blackness towards the football.

He hurled himself down on it, and quickly stuffed the muddy sphere into his backpack before scampering back to his mates.

When he threw the pack down, the soldiers cheerily fished inside for their football, only to pull out a severed German's head

A twist on the popular story about Xmas Day
games of football between German and English
troops, after which the two sides would pick
up their goal-posts and return to the more
enjoyable task of massacring each other. Selling
dummies one day, firing dum-dums the next.

Down and out

A story persists that during the First World War, at an airfield
in northern France, a Sopwith Camel was very late back from
a mission, and everyone assumed the plane and pilot were
lost.

Then just as all hope was abandoned, the hum of the
propellor preceded a sighting of the bi-plane, battle scarred
but flying normally. The plane manoeuvred into a descent
and made a perfect landing. Ground crew and an ambulance
rushed out to receive the flyer, but they weren't needed.

The pilot was dead, and had been so for at least two hours.

Marie Celeste eat your heart out. These days,
planes literally do fly themselves. [*See* Auto-
pirate, **Technophobia** *for proof*]

The amputee-escapee

During the First World War, there were many nasty stories
about the fate of captured Allied troops under German

control, but few were as revealing as this one, told by my grandad about one of his dad's fellow inmates.

This young, plucky lad was an officer who'd been caught at the Battle of the Somme, an horrific event which he was lucky to come out of alive. He was taken to a PoW camp, and immediately attempted an escape, hiding in a cart that passed through the site. A few hours later he was back in camp again, but after two weeks plotting made good his escape again, and was only caught when he fell down a rock face trying to elude a German patrol. He suffered horrible injuries to his legs and arms, and the camp hospital could do little to stop gangrene setting in. Soon, the doctor told him he'd have to have a leg removed. 'Herr Doktor,' said the young fellow, 'Could you do me the honour of having my amputated leg shipped back through the Red Cross to England. I'd like to be buried an Englishman through and through.'

The doctor acceded to his wish, and after the operation, saw to it that the leg was dispatched immediately to relatives back home.

Shortly, the other leg was marked down to go. The young Englishman made the same request, which was solemnly carried out.

But when the prisoner's arm was pronounced irretrievably damaged, and the fellow asked for it too to be sent back to Blighty, the doctor had grave news for him: 'I'm afraid I cannot send your arm back to England, mein Herr. The commandant is very strict about this. He thinks you are again trying to escape — this time bit by bit.'

Everyone loves a hero and military myths seem
to have a definite *Boys' Own* flavour to them;
men fired up with derring-do evoking the spirit
of Bulldog Drummond and *The Great Escape*.
Which makes the following story all the more
poignant . . .

Shot in the dark

There was, apparently, a particularly lucky Tommy during
the Second World War, known to his colleagues as 'Moggy'
Mellors because he seemed to have the nine lives of a cat,
all of which he made use of during his time at the front.

On one occasion he and two pals were walking, Indian
file, through a French village when a single sniper's bullet
scythed through the man in front and the man behind, but
somehow avoided Moggy in the middle altogether.

Another time he got lost wandering at night in a field in
Belgium, and it was only when he reached the other side and
held up a match to a sign on a tree which read 'Achtung!
Minefield!' that he found out he'd been rather fortunate
again.

In another episode, he fell in front of a German tank, but
the vehicle went straight over him and cleared him by a
matter of inches as he'd had his usual good fortune and fallen
into a crater.

Beyond that, he'd been caught by the enemy twice, only
for the Russians to liberate the camps he was in on both
occasions. In French towns on leave, his mates noted with
annoyance, he always seemed to get the *belle*-est

126

mademoiselles too. In short, Moggy was a spawny git.

Anyway, these stories and many other lucky escapes in his wartime career were being recalled by him and his pals at a regimental reunion party many years after the end of hostilities, as all the old Tommies gathered round a bonfire with the officers and celebrated.

Somehow Lady Luck wasn't with Moggy that evening, though. For the orderly who had been sweeping the ground around the bonfire had inadvertently brushed some ammunition in amongst the kindling at the bottom. As the night drew in and the laughter grew louder, the air was pierced by the crack of bullets shooting out of the roaring bonfire. Poor Moggy was shot straight through the heart, killing him instantly.

Spud-U-lob

My grandad's dad's company were being relieved in the trenches and falling back to recuperate. They'd been through a particularly bloody spell at the front and were taken to a small French town. The sergeant told them that as a special reward for their bravery they'd laid on some entertainment to promote greater harmony between the ranks. The tired troops were led into a field where there was an officer riding up and down on a horse.

They were given sacks of potatoes and told to throw the spuds at the officer − those who hit him most would get a prize. Now there was no love lost between the ranks in those days, and the troops pelted the spuds as hard as they possibly could.

The poor officer was getting battered black and blue, much to the soldier's enjoyment, until word went round that the real reason for the 'treat' was to see who were the most accurate and draft them into the grenade corps. In those days the grenades were extremely volatile and carried in a bag slung on the chest, making the job virtually suicidal.

Strangely, the soldiers' aim suddenly went haywire and none of them hit the target again. The puzzled sergeant waved away the officer, and to the troops' delight the grenade thrower vacancy remained unfilled.

Most wars have their myths, and the Falklands argie-bargie threw up a few new ones, mostly involving sheep. These woolly notions involved the beasts being mistaken either for Spanish-speaking Argentinians under cover of darkness or the SAS dressed up and roaming the island at will — or was it members of the Queen's 1st Foot and Mouth? Both these tales and more are covered fully in Rodney Dale's excellent book, *It's true . . . It happened to a friend*. Here's one Falklands myth you won't find there:

Crater disturbance

After an inaccurate British bombing raid on Port Stanley air-field, the Argentinians ran out on to the runways and unfurled huge plastic sheets with pictures of bomb craters on them, so that RAF reconnaissance thought they'd hit their target and didn't bother to raid it again.

The real reason the Argentinians lost the war was they spent too long making these plastic decoys and not long enough on laying plastic explosives.

> Thus the Argentinians join a long line of suspect
> decoy camouflage experts, ranging from the
> Greeks and their Trojan horse, through
> Mussolini's fleet of wooden aircraft and the
> Allies' inflatable tanks and rubber Lancasters
> (the ones that delivered the bouncing bomb),
> to cardboard shadows, used in the Gulf War
> on Iraqi airfields and meant to give the enemy
> the impression that Saddam had hundreds of
> jets under camouflage, silhouetted by the sun.
> Or was that just a Mirage?

War game pie

A friend who's a civvy pen-pusher at some secret naval intelligence joint recently had to go on one of those survival courses up in the Brecon Beacons, run by the marines. He was very apprehensive at having his mettle tested by the big macho marines, as the nearest he got to physical exercise was taking the top off his biro.

Anyway, the course started off with a pleasant surprise. The shaven-headed hard-nut sergeant gave them all a cuddly pet bunny and asked them to give it a name. The shiny-arse named it after his mother-in-law, Mavis, and took to it straight away.

The week itself was horrendous, assault course after assault course, forced marches through driving rain, night manoeuvres, and two days orienteering alone way out in the wilderness without a tent, food or drink.

When they got back to the base, half dead, having lugged the docile little rabbit around all week, feeding it and looking after it, the sergeant offered them a choice that would chill any Englishman to the marrow: kill the rabbit, skin it and eat it — or do the whole week again.

Heat-seeking rissole

All new-fangled devices and their unknown properties seem to bring out the worst paranoia in us, and this is particularly true of secretive military hardware, around which numerous myths have been spun. Perhaps more than any other, the evocative idea of a 'heat-seeking' missile has fired the public imagination, and the weapon has endeared itself to the myth-telling public at large.

One story concerns a military exercise taking place on Salisbury Plain. All the brass hats are there to witness a demonstration of a new, ultra-sensitive heat-seeking weapon. But when the missile is fired at a tank five hundred metres away on the plain, it swerves off and flies towards the generals, narrowly missing their cars and blowing up a mobile canteen, where the NAAFI cook is doing a fry-up for the hungry troops.

> So much for 'smart' bombs. And anyway, if
> a bomb's so bleeding clever, why does it want
> to be in the army?

Flipperin' dangerous

During the fifties, the American navy experimented with using dolphins and porpoises to place magnetic bombs on the underside of enemy ships. The project was soon abandoned because the cuddly creatures kept coming back, with the ticking explosives still strapped to their heads when the mines wouldn't stick.

There are tragic echoes there of the sad story of the white Beluga whale adopted by Turkish villagers in the spring of 1992. The playful fellow, frolicking around a fishing port thousands of miles from its Baltic home, had excaped from its Russian navy captors, who were using it in military experiments. But it knew too much, and the iron fist of red oppression . . . sorry, the newly liberated state, exercising its democratic rights, tracked the beleaguered Beluga down, and trawled him off back to the labs.

MYTHELLANEOUS

Military

★ Churchill was going to cover the Channel with crude oil and set light to it if Hitler tried to invade

★ Modern weapons have pin-point accuracy from hundreds of miles away

★ Paratroopers know how to kill people with their bare hands in over fifty different ways

★ When Wrens and seamen shared ships during the Gulf War, they were at it all the time

★ Battles are won on the playing fields of Eton

★ Angels used to appear quite regularly to Allied soldiers at Mons in the First World War

★ If you write your name on a bullet and keep it in your pocket, you'll never get shot

★ The first ever tanks had asses inside them, and built-in nose-bags (now they've dispensed with the nose-bags)

★ The American army has the best pack-lunches on manoeuvres; the British have the worst

★ At night, snipers get you if you light three ciggies from one match: one to see it, one to take aim, and one to shoot

★ What the youth of this country needs is a damn good war

★ During the Second World War, soldiers were quite often saved when bullets hit their cigarette cases

★ You don't have to be able to swim to join the navy

★ There are so many dodgy characters on American aircraft carriers that the captain has to have a round-the-clock armed bodyguard

TRAVEL SICKNESS

The perils lurking in foreign parts

The British hate to see other people enjoying themselves, so it's not surprising there are so many urban myths about dream holidays that go horribly wrong. Whether you're a broad abroad or just incontinent on the continent, it's all aboard for a first-class cruise into troubled waters, where most of the travellers come home with only tears for souvenirs. These over-the-top overseas odysseys may kick sand in the face of common sense but underlying that is a pernicious xenophobia, a basic distrust of foreigners and all their parts . . .

The ring of confidence

A couple I know went on holiday one year to a hotel in the Mediterranean. They were having a great time until, halfway through their stay, their room was broken into. Mysteriously, nothing had been stolen, though their drawers had been rifled through.

Slightly unnerved they nevertheless enjoyed the rest of their holiday. When they got home, thoroughly relaxed, one of the first things they did was to put their films in for developing — mementoes of the happy vacation.

But the shots they got back provided something of an unpleasant shock. In amongst the pictures of the couple on the beach and in the hotel bar were some revealing snaps showing a rear aspect of the would-be burglars. They were naked, except for the holiday couple's toothbrushes, shoved head-first up their hairy bottoms.

> And remember, the break-in happened *halfway* through the holiday . . .

The burning deck

A friend's brother won a sweepstake at work and decided to blow it all on a Caribbean cruise. He was having a whale of a time, dancing and drinking 'til the early hours every night, flirting with women and generally having the time of his life. One day he got up particularly late, about lunchtime, with a stinking hangover, crawled out of bed; dragged on his trunks and, slipping on his shades, stumbled out into the bright Mediterranean sunshine.

Because it was so late most of the sun-loungers had been taken by Germans, and there seemed to be nowhere for him to crash out. Luckily, he found a nice sunny spot on the deck, lay down on the warm bare metal bulkhead, and dropped off.

He woke up in agony a couple of hours later to find the blistering midday sun had melted his skin and his body was glued to the scorching steel deck.

Odd customs

A mate of mine's dad is an airline pilot. He worked the New York—London run for BA for years and remembers one incident which still makes him chuckle.

He had flown a Jumbo into Heathrow, and when the passengers had disembarked, one of the stewardesses found a little carved box under one of the seats. When she opened it, she found a suspicious-looking powder inside.

Customs staff arrived immediately and one opened the box, licking his little finger before dipping it into the powder and putting it into his mouth to taste it.

'Well, it's not a narcotic,' he said, efficiently. Just then, an elderly lady came along the aisle and asked the stewardess if she'd happened to come across a small casket containing her husband's ashes.

[*See also* Atlantic potion, **Friends and Relations**]

Out of the fishing boat, into the fire

The boss of my friend's firm was a lover of the good things in life, and one of the best, according to him, was the South of France, particularly the Camargue. He spent a lot of time there and absolutely adored fishing. One baking hot summer day, he determined to hire a rowing boat and go fishing out in a lake. He found an idyllic, deserted stretch of water, but there were no hire facilities. Luckily, among the rushes he found an old boat that still floated okay and slipped out into the middle of the lake for a fish and a kip holding his rod.

Unhappily, as often happens in the region during hot summers, a huge forest fire blew up a few miles away. The local authorities were alerted and sent for the crop-spray planes to douse the fire with water.

The planes apparently work by flying low over water and scooping the stuff into their holds, then dumping it over the fire.

Our man was still in the land of nod when a plane approached his tiny boat, gathering him up along with several hundred gallons of H_2O, and dropped him, miraculously unharmed, on to the scorching scrub below.

Sun basting

A friend of my auntie's, who in her youth had been a cracking bit of stuff, was getting on in years but still a looker. She liked to take care of her appearance and loved to have a deep bronze tan to show off her long 'blonde' hair. Her husband usually booked a holiday in Greece about springtime to make sure she looked good in her bikini in the back garden, topping up her tan.

However, one year, due to the Tories' recession, they'd been a bit skint and had to miss out on their week in the Med. When the summer months came around she wanted to build up her tan quicker than usual.

She'd seen those sun-reflector-type things that accelerate tanning in her catalogue, and decided to have a go herself on the cheap. So she knocked up a home-made reflector out of aluminium baking foil and a coat-hanger, and erected the contraption round her sun-lounger in the back garden. The day was a real scorcher, so she lay down for some serious sun worship.

But when her husband came home from work he found her lying in the garden, cooked through like a goose . . .

Legless in Gaza

My auntie's dad was travelling solo around what was then Palestine just after the Second World War in a jeep, but injured his leg in a fall in the hills.

Unable to drive, it was several days before he managed to hobble to find help, and he was taken to a field hospital, set up to administer everyday medicine to local villagers near Gaza.

Although they didn't really have the facilities, they thought it would be too late to save the leg (gangrene was setting in) if he was transferred to the nearest town, so they decided to operate immediately.

Sadly, there was some hoohah involving a local bigwig's

son and some goats which spilled over into the 'operating theatre'. In the confusion, the wrong leg was amputated.

Fortunately, because of their terrible error, the staff worked extra hard on his remaining leg, and managed to save it.

The flame-haired toupée of Thika

There was a young advertising executive I worked with who we were all convinced used to wear a spikey Rod Stewart-style 'piece', or toupée, of reddish hue to match his remaining locks. He was a supremely confident geezer, but no one could bring themselves to quiz him about his syrup-of-fig, and it stayed the topic of debate whenever he left the room.

Last year, though, he went on holiday to Kenya, staying in a beach hut camp near Mombasa, and told us all a harrowing story when he got back. It was out of season and there were only two other couples on site apart from the ad. exec. and his wife and the security guards.

Halfway through a fantastic holiday, they were woken by a knock on their hut door. It was two in the morning, and not being able to find a pair of his own, the adman slipped on a pair of his wife's knickers and opened the door. Outside were around fifteen huge Masai with machine guns and machetes. They'd knocked out both guards and quite courteously asked for all the couple's belongings.

The bloke stood around in the knickers while they rifled through everything they owned, stealing watches, whisky (which they set about drinking right away), clothes, anything hard to get in Kenya. He was terrified they might hurt him, or, worse, start on his wife.

But after an hour of terror, the Masai left the hut and sat outside drinking. The adman was so relieved, at first he said *'Asanti sana'* − Swahili for 'Thank you' − to them. But as time went by, he became more nervous listening to their increasingly drunken shouts.

As it happened, they soon disappeared. The bloke looked to see what was left. All their clothes had been taken. All he had left were the knickers he'd been wearing − and he'd soiled them three times.

As he told us this, we looked on enthralled − partly at the horrific story, and partly at the vision of a Masai warrior proudly sporting his new fiery red Rod headpiece around Happy Valley − our colleague had returned to work with his head completed shaved as a cover-up.

'Be'ind you!'

A Plymouth couple went on a trip to Paris, driving via ferry to the romantic French capital, and quickly finding their way to the hotel by twilight.

Once there, the problem was finding somewhere to park. They'd heard about the infamous Parisian 'listening parking' where the driver backs up until he hears a crunch, and were determined to give a good account of British drivers.

Eventually, they found somewhere down an awkward, congested side road. The bloke was driving and backing up gingerly into the space, but found it hard to see.

It happened that a passing Parisian noticed their 'GB' sticker and the difficulties they were having, and ran over to direct them, gesticulating.

'You've a metre be'ind you,' he shouted.

So the bloke backed up a little more. The local waved his hands and repeated: 'You've a metre be'ind you!' So the driver edged back even further.

The Parisian waved and shouted again, this time somewhat impatiently: 'You've a metre be'ind you!!'

So the bloke put his foot down and reversed sharply back. CRUNCH! The Parisian shook his head, tutting, and tapped on the window, pointing to a mangled metal post bent over behind the car.

'I told you that you 'ad a meter be'ind you!'

Handy for the beach

A young couple were among the first Brits to travel to beautiful Gambia, West Africa, when it opened up to tourists. They were bowled over by the friendliness of the locals, the fantastic weather and the wonderful, unspoilt beaches.

One day, as the man was swimming in the sea, the woman was flat out topping up her tan, half asleep.

After she'd done her front, she flopped over on to her stomach and stretched her arms out. As she did so, she made contact with cold flesh and, thinking it was her boyfriend straight out of the sea, looked over. It was a stiff hand, sticking up out of the sand, and it belonged to a body, also there in the sand.

As it turned out, it is the custom among some people in the region to bury a person where they die. This person drowned, but they would never bury someone at sea where the scavenging fish could get them . . .

140

Swiss rolled

One of my mates worked in Lagos, Nigeria, for a number of years. It's a pretty rough city according to him, and he used to tell a story that supported his case.

He was approached one day by a tearful, middle-aged Swiss couple, who related to him their sorry tale. They'd arrived the same day in Nigeria, on what they'd dreamed would be the holiday of a lifetime. They'd saved up for ages and managed to book flights going right across Africa, with Lagos their first port of call. All the rest of their life-savings they packed with them as cash and traveller's cheques for convenience.

They'd efficiently read loads of guide-books beforehand, so when they arrived at scorching hot Lagos airport, they knew that they should look for a taxi that displayed a licence and had a number plate, as there were loads of unregulated drivers who would rip you off as soon as look at you.

Clutching their city guide-book, they scanned the cab rank and picked the best looking vehicle, a beaten-up old Peugeot 504 with a number plate and licence. They lugged their heavy suitcases over to it.

The cabbie was a friendly geezer, asked them where they were from, and warmly welcomed them to Nigeria. Then he took their cases and shut them securely in the boot, saying, 'Keep the windows shut when we go through town, because kids try and reach in to grab your jewellery.' They took his good advice and thanked him for his trouble.

On the journey to their hotel, the driver gave them plenty more useful tips: good restaurants to eat in, sights to see, places to avoid and the like. By the time they reached their destination, the Swiss couple were thanking him profusely, and getting really excited at the city they were about to explore.

Outside the hotel, the taxi-driver kept the engine running and started fumbling around under the dashboard for a pen. He suggested the couple might want to get their things out of the boot while he wrote down some of the addresses he'd told them about.

They both got out and walked round to the boot. But the driver slammed his foot down and the taxi sped away from them, still laden with their cases, money, plane tickets and clothes – everything they had except the heavy European tweeds they were left standing in.

When they strained to catch the rogue's number plate, all they saw was a filthy rag taped over it, flapping away in the grimy exhaust fumes.

This is a universal travel story, and everyone claims to have met an acquaintance of the impecunious victims, but Nigerians seem to be getting a particularly bad press at the moment, what with all the financial fraud stories doing the rounds. Speaking of which, a quick aside about Nigerian business practice in the mid-seventies. Apparently, during the country's oil boom, many entrepreneurs ordered tankers full of liquid cement from European companies to lay the foundations for Lagos' new developments. Unfortunately, oil prices collapsed in 1974, and the fleets of cement tankers moored up at Lagos harbour only to find no trace at all of the person who made the deal. So the ships, sometimes as many as fourteen, would remain moored offshore for weeks, their cargo slowly setting.

Board and logic

There was a young lad at a prep school in Sussex who was always jealous of other kids flying home at weekends when he had to stay boarding.

So one day, when there was a study day, he slipped away from school and made his way to Gatwick. He had no idea that aeroplanes went to different destinations, and just thought that any one would take him home to Morocco. Aware that he didn't have a passport or ticket, he realised he had to be a bit devious.

So what he did was wait for a large family with lots of children to approach the check-in, and when the commotion they caused had passed and they were well through, he ran up shouting: 'Mummy, mummy, wait for me!'

The check-in people were taken in by this small boy, and he was allowed through with a smile. He did exactly the same thing with the security checks — no problem either.

In fact, he'd got as far as Paris, where the flight stopped first en route to Lagos, Nigeria, before the staff realised they had a stowaway on board.

The next three stories play upon our basic fear
of being exposed in public places whilst at large

in strange parts. In these particular exotic escapades, the red-faced embarrassment remains long after the suntan has faded.

The naked ski-girl

A friend was on a skiing holiday in the French Alps. She was having a brilliant time, the weather was fantastic and the snow just peachy. She was a pretty experienced skier and one day decided to go off exploring the slopes by herself. The snow was lovely and compacted with a nice little blow on top.

She was just traversing down an especially fine piste when she was caught short – too much *après ski* the night before. There was no chance of getting back to the lodge in time, and as no one else was around she decided to do it there and then.

Carefully, she unzipped her one-piece designer ski suit and peeled it off down to the knees.

But in the middle of going, she started to move. She'd inadvertently done the 'snow plough' with her skis and was soon hurtling out of control half-naked down the slope.

She ended up in a heap at the bottom of the mountain and was taken to hospital suffering from over-exposure.

In hospital she was relating this story to the man in the bed next to her, in traction with two broken legs, who creased up laughing. When she finished, she asked him how he'd sustained his injuries.

Apparently, he'd been thundering down the slopes when a naked girl on skis had hurtled past, distracting him, and he'd crashed into a tree.

Private viewing

An old friend and his girlfriend went on the holiday of a life-time, touring around the Indian sub-continent for six months.

At Christmas time, they found themselves in romantic, dusty Agra. They'd just had a wonderful day looking round the amazing Taj Mahal, and in the balm of the evening set their hearts on a candlelit meal for two in a cosy local restaurant.

The restaurant was a bit rough and rickety, and very quiet, but the staff were really friendly and the food was delicious. They were having the time of their life.

Towards the end of the dinner, the young woman called one of the attentive boy waiters over and asked if the restaurant had a toilet, half expecting him to say no.

The waiter smiled hugely and pointed to an eight-foot-high curtained cubicle, towards the end of the seating area. The woman left the table, brushed her way through the drapes of the makeshift lavatory, and sat down on a shaky stool above the tin receptable.

While she was at her doings, she was sure she heard the sound of chairs being scuffed around. But she carried on, until she heard a sudden rustling above her head.

Then she looked up to see a host of smiling waiters' faces leering inquisitively over the top of the cubicle at her scantily clad body.

Rollerballs

A friend of a bloke I play snooker with went to Amsterdam for a couple of days, intending to have a wild old time, and take full advantage of the local hospitality.

One stoned afternoon he went to a theatre where there were a number of beautiful naked women on stage, performing tricks on roller skates. The audience were loving it.

For one sequence they needed a member from the audience, and this bloke, ogling at the front, was dragged up by them. They took him to the top of a steep ramp, stripped him starkers and put roller skates on him.

Then a number of the women positioned themselves at the bottom of the ramp and bent over invitingly. He was getting really worked up as he was pushed down the slope towards them.

He shot off down the ramp, and the women jumped out of his way at the last moment, pulled back some curtains and left him to hurtle through open doors into the sunny street outside.

> More variations exist around this old chestnut
> than there are tulips in Holland. One particular
> favourite features saucy sailors on leave in
> Portsmouth.

Long-haul lamb

A Glaswegian TV producer was visited by her parents, farmers from the Western Isles. They caught a plane to Glasgow and arrived on time.

But at baggage reclaim, they were concerned to see that one of their items was missing. It was half a lamb from their farm, straight out the freezer, that they'd put in a cardboard box, tied up with string. They told airline officials and when the staff couldn't trace the package, the couple were assured that they would be informed the moment it was traced.

The pair complained strongly, because the lamb was frozen when they packed it, and might go off if it stood around too long. They left their daughter's home telephone number and continued on there themselves.

The next morning, they received a phone call from the airline saying that they should expect the package to be delivered a little later. Sure enough, the missing box was duly delivered. Attached to the box was a note, apologising and explaining there had been a clerical mix-up.

Apparently, when the lamb arrived at Glasgow airport, it had been mistakenly put straight on a jet to London Heathrow. When it arrived there, another bureaucratic balls-up meant it was immediately placed on a Concorde flight to JFK in New York.

Fortunately, the handlers at JFK recognised the error and put the well-travelled lamb straight back on the same Concorde to Heathrow, from where it was finally returned to Glasgow, still frozen. The family gratefully had it for dinner that very night.

Welcome to Dallas

An Englishman on his first trip to Dallas, Texas, found himself the focus of attention of a liberated, rich and beautiful young woman — they love the accent apparently. She was all over him like a rash, and he was just over the moon. Slightly overwhelmed by her forward nature, he nevertheless invited her back to his hotel room and was thrilled when she accepted.

As soon as they were in the room, she whipped her kit off and dived between the sheets. He quickly followed suit, even removing his socks. When it came to the point of no return, he, being a New Man, instinctively fumbled in his jeans pocket for a latex life-saver.

'Uh-oh,' said the Dallas lady. 'Bare-back riders only with me, cowboy!' So they got stuck in as nature intended.

The man awoke the next day to find that his lover had slipped away. Smiling and humming to himself, he opened the curtains and ordered breakfast.

It was only when he went into the bathroom to draw himself a bath that he noticed, scrawled on the mirror in gaudy red lipstick, 'Welcome to the AIDS Club sucker! Have a nice day!'

> Of course, before Aids, the same story welcomed the victim to the 'Herpes' club. And before that . . . whatever was the sexual phobia of the day.

MYTHELLANEOUS

Travel

★ Greek holiday apartment blocks look like they're only half built, because it means the owner doesn't have to pay tax

★ It's bad luck to cross the equator twice in one day

★ Bikinis are illegal in Turkey

★ Postcards of the Queen make good bartering currency anywhere in the world

★ Americans think Britain is an island just off New York

★ Take a pint of your own blood in a flask for emergencies

★ You can sell your blood in Dubai

★ In India, they nod when they mean 'no' and shake their heads to say 'yes'

★ It is illegal not to wear a shirt in Monaco

★ You've got more chance of being arrested in Spain than anywhere else in the world

★ In Arab countries: it is rude not to burp in appreciation after a meal; if you like something, they give it to you; the biggest insult is to show someone the soles of your feet

★ Koreans sleep standing up for at least two or three years of their lives

★ Fijian pearl divers have their ear-drums burst at an early age so they can go down deeper

NEW YORK STORIES

Maggoty myths from the Big Apple

The ugly side of America the Beautiful is New York, portrayed as a sort of loopy, hi-tech Babylon, where sex is cheap and crime costs lives, and it always gets a bad press from myth-tellers. We've come across a particularly odd selection of paranoid stories set there where the American dream turns into a nightmare . . .

Bombed out at JFK

When he arrived at JFK airport, New York, for the return flight to London, my cousin's mate was surprised to find the place swarming with police cars, sirens wailing, lights flashing.

It could only be a bomb scare, especially as it was just after the Ayatollah had issued his *fatwa* against Salman Rushdie, and the author was rumoured to be about to arrive Stateside for a lecture tour. As it was, the focus of all the security was the London-bound plane and there were extremely thorough baggage checks for all passengers on the flight.

After four hours tense hanging around, they were finally allowed on the aeroplane. All settled in, engines roaring for take-off, there was suddenly a rather disturbing announcement: 'Good evening ladies and gentlemen, this is your Captain speaking. We apologise for the long delay. This is due to police finding a bomb on board . . .'

The kidney burglar

A friend of a friend was on holiday in New York for the first time and, buzzing at the prospect of enjoying the thrills and spills of the world's most exciting city, the Big Apple, checked into his hotel then went out on the razzle. He soon found himself in one of the less salubrious areas, Queens, in a typical New York bar, set up for a night of margaritas and who knows what.

After a few stiff ones, he got talking to an attractive Hispanic woman. She was so vivacious and friendly that he began to think he might break his NYC duck on the first night — and with a real New Yoik chica! When she invited him back to her place he leapt at the chance, though he was so drunk he could hardly stand.

From there on he couldn't remember anything else until the next day. He woke up in a strange bed alone and was struck by a sharp pain in his midriff. Looking down he was taken aback to see a newly sewn wound on his side and rushed out to a hospital, where they immediately gave him an X-ray. He was numbed when they told him that one of his kidneys had been surgically stolen.

> There is medical evidence to support this story in the number of cases of people from developing countries who have recently been willing to sell parts of their body to medical practitioners in the West — in particular the celebrated case of a Harley Street surgeon who had a racket going buying kidneys from impoverished Turks. We've even heard of people selling their eyes in India, and liver donors in Albania. What a weird world . . .

The Empire State escape

Apparently, a man once fell from the top of the Empire State building and survived, because he had the good fortune to land on a passing truck full of mattresses.

'Hit the deck, lady'

Some friends of my parents' were on holiday in America, doing a fly-drive package, and decided to spend a few days in New York. They'd been out on the town, done a show on Broadway and had an Italian meal on the Lower East Side. They'd been a bit nervous at first about being in the Big Apple, after seeing all those violent shoot-'em-up cop shows on TV, but now they were feeling quite at home and the service was fantastic.

They drove back to the hotel, pulled up in the basement car park and were waiting for the lift up to reception. It was pretty dark and spooky, the lights were flickering and water dripping, just like the 'Deep Throat' scenes in *All the President's Men*.

Just then a huge black man with a Rottweiler loomed out of the shadows. The lift came and the couple scuttled in. But the huge figure sped up and got inside the lift with his grizzly hound just before the doors closed. Immediately, the black man shouted 'Hit the deck, lady' and the petrified couple threw themselves down on the floor, thrusting all their money upon him, before the lift doors opened and they scarpered out.

Obviously, the incident tainted their stay, and the next day they went to reception to check out. To their surprise, the receptionist explained that a man had already settled their hotel bill, and handed them an envelope.

Inside was all the money they'd thrown at the 'mugger', and a note saying: 'I'm real sorry about scaring you yesterday, and I hope this has made it up to you. By the way, "Lady" is the name of my dog . . .'

In some verisons we've heard, the misunder-
stood black man is said to be none other than
film star comedian Eddie Murphy, or some
other Afro-American notable like Mike Tyson
(honestly, who'd be frightened of him?).
Sometimes he's said to shout the alternative
line, 'Get down, bitch.'

The buggering Bronx Batman

A friend of a friend called Robin was enjoying a well-earned
holiday in New York. He was having a great time in the
twenty-four-hour city, he'd seen all the sights: the Empire
State building, Times Square, Broadway, and of course the
Statue of Liberty. But after a few days he was feeling a bit
lonesome, so he decided to go out clubbing in Greenwich
Village and try his luck.

He managed to blag his way into a new hot and hip
nightspot but wasn't doing too well. In fact, he hadn't had
a nibble all night, until a fabulously attractive older woman
caught his eye. She came over to him and they started talking.

He couldn't believe his luck; here he was talking to a
beautiful, intelligent, witty native New Yorker, who found
Englishmen irresistible. After a few more drinks they kissed
– and what a kiss. Then she suggested going back to her
place to get better acquainted. He didn't need asking twice.

They caught a yellow cab and took off. She was so randy
she couldn't leave him alone. He was gagging for it.

When they got to her penthouse, she practically ravaged
him the moment they were through the door, then whispered

a suggestion to try something kinky. He nodded furiously. She peeled off her clothes, undressed him completely, and led him to the bedroom where she tied him spread-eagled and face down on the bed.

Then at the crucial moment, a male accomplice burst out of the wardrobe, dressed as Batman, and took him forcibly from behind.

UNDER THE KNIFE

Mythical medical mayhem

These nasty narratives play on our deep-seated fear that
you're nothing without your health, our sneaking belief in
superstitious 'old wives' tales', and percolating mistrust of
the quack Kildares who are supposed to look after us even
when we're out for the count. These malignant health records
pare to the bone the cut and thrust of hospital practice, where
the only real casualty is the truth. If laughter is the best
medicine, then these urban myths have got to be the finest
prescription — if only for a sick sense of humour. For every
technological breakthrough in the medical field, there's a
sceptic with a poisoned mind ready to spin another morbid
and worrying yarn. They'll have you in stitches . . .

Gone to seed

A grubby young lad we knew vaguely at school was apparently sitting at the table eating his tea one evening, when his mother noticed that, as usual, his nose needed attention. 'Go and wipe your nose — and use your hanky,' she boomed. 'But it's not running, Mummy,' he replied.

So his mother called him over, and took her own hanky out ready for action. But when he sat on her lap, she could see, to her horror, that it was actually a small green leaf that was protruding from his nostril. She gave it a little tug, and teased out the end of what was clearly a tomato plant. He had sneezed while eating a tomato some months back, and one of the seeds must have got lodged.

The boy was rushed to hospital where doctors immediately examined him and operated. 'It's a good job we caught it in time,' said one to the mother afterwards. 'A few more weeks and the plant would have penetrated his brain.'

In common with many of the stories in this section, the tomato implant myth is one of those the tabloids fondly turn to during the so-called 'silly season', year after year. It's got just enough horror, just enough weirdness, and just enough credibility as a medical phenomenon to do the business. Look out for these little stories in the papers; they're normally about five lines long, with no names, a vague geographical location (often in the Third World) and no byline. Bored sub-editors who need to fill space love 'em

The farm hand

A friend of mine told me about this bloke in his village, a farmworker, who's known more for his muscle than his mental agility. Apparently, one September the farmworker was labouring in the field, driving his combine harvester. He left the cab and for some reason tampered with the machine while it was still going – checking for obstructions or something. Anyway, he strayed too close to the flashing blades and his left arm was hacked off.

In pain, but undaunted, he shoved the severed limb inside his rough farmworkers' jacket, continued driving one-handed, quickly finished harvesting the field, and drove all the way to the county hospital in the combine, parking in some of the head consultants' spaces, and demanding the arm be sewn back on.

Re-animation

When I was a nipper, my mate's mum was a nurse, and she reckons she saw some pretty queer things in her time at a hospital in Kent. On one occasion, she was taking some bedpans to be emptied and took a short cut through the mortuary. As she walked in she noticed there was a fresh cadaver on the slab, unattended.

She was just crossing the room when the corpse sat bolt upright and yelled 'BAH' before falling back down again.

Ever the unflappable professional, she put the hair-raising experience down to the build-up of internal gases released by decomposition, but us impressionable kids were sure it was something far more sinister.

Aorta know better

This doctor friend told me about a top Harley Street surgeon who's a bit of a joker — wears a spinning bow-tie, acts like Leslie Philips in the *Carry On* films, that sort of fellow. Anyway, what he most enjoys is to 'blood' young doctors and nurses in operating techniques. Literally, in fact, for during open-heart surgery he would always make sure the débutants stood close to him. Then he'd unclip the patient's main valve, and squirt his assistant in the face with a warm gush of arterial blood.

She never even knew she was pregnant . . .

At the girls' school just up the road from ours, there was a big-boned girl in the fourth form who was feeling very dodgy one day. She went to the toilet, and a few minutes later gave birth to a bouncing baby boy. And she never even knew she was pregnant . . .

Flushed with embarrassment

There was a portly old woman who lived in Wigan, who had an outside toilet with no seat on it. One day she went out through the garden to use it and wearily plonked herself down. The force of her descent created a vacuum between

her behind and the porcelain, and she was stuck fast for
hours. Eventually, the fire brigade was called and had to
demolish the brick outhouse around her and then carry her
through the house, past inquisitive neighbours and into a
waiting ambulance, still astride the latrine.

[*See also* Going down, **Friends and Relations**]

Four eyes only

An optometrist friend knows a nice story that did the rounds
a few years back about two brothers who go to the optician.
The older boy has been checked and fitted and has come in
to collect his specs; the younger sibling is in for his fitting,
and is really upset at having to wear goggles. When his senior
comes back into the waiting room, the little lad is heartened
because the glasses look really good.

But when he sits down in the chair and the 'fun' optometrist
puts a cornflake packet, with an eye hole cut out, over the
boy's head to test the eyes' relative strength, he bursts into
tears. The optician stops immediately and asks the sobbing
boy what's the matter. 'I want some like my brother's!' blubs
the boy.

Scal-pal

A mate who was a medical student at Newcastle University
tells a story about one of his colleagues who was at a human
dissection lecture.

Bodies 'left to science' are always transported well away from their locality, but when the shrouds were pulled back to reveal a fresh body on the slab with the skin partially removed, one young woman fainted. When revived, she disclosed that the body was that of her former fiancé, who'd died some weeks earlier in an horrific motorcycle crash in Wales.

The hair nest

A girl in the town my mum was born in grew her hair into a beehive, as was the fashion in the Fifties. But this girl wasn't renowned for her fastidious personal hygiene, and as the hairstyle began to get dirty and saggy, her schoolmates began to notice little movements in her hair and a funny clicking sound.

At first the kids thought it was lice, which were quite common at the time, but when it came to school medical time, the nurse discovered that a colony of cockroaches had taken up residence in her once trendy locks. Later, the story got around that the infestation was actually beetles, and that they'd been boring into the girl's ear, gnawing away at her brain . . .

> Bizarre as that perennial apocryphal hair story may be, we've got something to equal it. A friend is always obsessive about removing clippings of hair after having his hair cut. Because, as he says, if you let the little ends stay on your skin, they take root, and you end up with a full growth on your back, shoulders and inside your ears. Elton John, Terry Wogan take note . . .

The back eye

My uncle's mate has a glass eye of piercing blue hue. He used to relish an entertaining party trick, but stopped performing it for reasons which will become all too clear in a moment. He would take the eye out of its socket and slip it into his mouth, shocking people by parting his lips so that the eye stared out at them disconcertingly.

However, one time in the pub he was doing just that, but started laughing so much that he choked on the glass eye and finally swallowed it. When he consulted a doctor, the medic told him there was nothing to be done: 'Nature will have to take its course.' Several days later, the same doctor was treated to the sight of the blue eye lodged in the prankster's painful sphincters, staring out blandly.

False leg fight

Two football fans from Birmingham were travelling down to an away match in the early seventies to watch their team, Tottenham, play in a local derby at Arsenal. As most people know, there's no love lost between the two teams, and this was especially the case in the seventies, when unpleasant violent incidents were common. As Tottenham fans from Birmingham are fairly rare, the two lads came down on an ordinary train without a police escort, wearing their team colours with pride.

They needed to catch the tube up to Arsenal, which meant a change at King's Cross. So they headed through the labyrinths to the Piccadilly Line. The station was fairly quiet until the lads heard chanting echoing behind them in the tunnels. At first, they couldn't tell whether it was Tottenham fans, Arsenal fans or whoever, but they sounded aggressive and they were getting closer. Then a rowdy bunch of Arsenal skinheads rampaged round the corner. Both Brummies tried to run away before any trouble flared, but one of the lads had a limp and couldn't keep up.

Both were caught and fell to the floor in a hail of kicks and punches. The bloke who had the limp was getting a real kicking, when quite unexpectedly his artificial leg shot out of his trousers and scuttled across the floor. One of the skinheads screamed, 'Jesus, you've kicked his bloody leg off!' and they fled back up the tunnel in terror.

The tooth fairy

An elderly lady who lived near us had been deaf in one ear since she was a little girl before the war. She had always shunned a hearing aid, and just accepted that she was a little mutton. It wasn't until she was in hospital for another complaint that an X-ray revealed an odd cause of her deafness: there was a small milk tooth lodged firmly in her inner ear. She'd always wondered why she never got any money after she left it under her pillow for the tooth fairy . . .

Medium-wave molars

A Leicester woman of advanced years went to the doctor complaining of a tiny ringing in her ears that was stopping her sleeping and was generally exasperating. The doctor at first thought it was tinnitus — 'white noise' of the inner ear. But when he came to examine her closely, he could hear the phenomenon himself — coming from her mouth. Eventually he discovered that recent fillings were acting as a medium-wave receiver. Even worse, it was picking up Radio 2.

Apparently, the new metal they use in fillings picks up teletext! Now there's a thing.

Sticky situation

A friend of my workmate's auntie had to pop into hospital for a check-up of a gynaecological nature and was quite nervous at the prospect. She was sitting in the waiting room feeling extremely jittery and in desperate need of the toilet, her nerves having affected her waterworks. So she wandered off in search of a convenience, which was happily nearby. Relieved, she reached out for the paper only to find that, due to NHS cuts, the roll was finished. But opening her handbag, she rooted around, dredged out a tissue and in desperation used that.

When she got back, her name was called. Shortly she was surrounded by inquisitive medical students and a crusty old consultant who asked her to open wide. Incredibly embarrassed, she nevertheless did as bid. There were gasps and guffaws from the students, so the consultant came down hard on one giggling youth:

'What's the matter, never seen one before?'

'Yes,' he spluttered, 'but never with a stamp on it.'

Wagging it

A friend of my uncle's owns a really mad mongrel dog, a proper Heinz 57; not dangerous, but nutty as a fruit cake. It's got one of those wagging tails that only mongrels have: always whipping from side to side, knocking ornaments off shelves and that kind of thing.

Anyway, one day the dog was leaping about in the kitchen while the bloke was scraping its dinner out of a tin. Unfortunately the crazed beast caught the table-cloth and dragged their best china on to the hard tile floor, smashing the lot.

The bloke was so furious that he lashed out at the mutt with his foot, but missed, slipped and fell down hard. He landed heavily, right on his coccyx – the small triangular bone at the base of his spine. It was awfully sore for days and still throbbing a week later, so he went to the doctor.

The quack was stunned. The blow had somehow triggered a primitive growth hormone and the bone was growing into what it had been in primeval times – a prehensile tail. In a queer throwback, the bloke ended up with a stumpy tail-like growth. He could wag it and everything . . .

Given the slip

A friend of my girlfriend left school and became what he'd always wanted to be, a police pathologist.

On one occasion the boys in blue called him out to the scene of a suspicious incident, seeking his professional opinion. Kitted out in his best doctor's outfit, tweed suit with white coat and coloured biros in the top pocket, he marched up the gravel path clutching his black bag of tricks.

The run-down old house seemed to have been stripped bare and his firm footsteps echoed through the empty building. He entered the living-room to meet detectives on the case.

They were standing by an emaciated body. It had obviously been lying there for some time, as all the fat from the corpse had run out and set in an inch-deep pool on the lino. Understandably, the CID weren't overly keen to touch the body, but the pathologist needed to take samples and couldn't turn the stiff on his own.

Gingerly, wearing medical rubber gloves, they took hold of the corpse and heaved, but the human lard was extremely slippery. They all lost their footing and fell heavily into the congealed fat, slipping and slithering around for several minutes. A scene not unworthy of the *Keystone Kops*.

Eye eye

A bloke was having an operation on a detached retina, when apparently the anaesthetic ran out and he regained consciousness. One eye could see perfectly normally, but the other was lying on his cheek, staring straight at a glinting scalpel blade.

It could happen . . .

Cavity wall filling

A friend of my sister-in-law went to have a tooth pulled at the dentist. The cack-handed quack was hopeless though, and was cutting and pulling around for about twenty minutes before stopping and saying, 'I'm afraid I can't do this job. You'll have to go to a dental hospital. There's one a few miles away.'

So the poor woman, half-anaesthetised, had to get a bus across town to the hospital. The dental surgeon took one look in her mouth and operated straight away.

Afterwards, she said to the woman. 'That other dentist hacked away half your top jaw. Whatever you do, don't sneeze with your mouth shut from now on, because the bone is so thin, you'll blow a hole from your mouth through into your sinuses.'

This one definitely *is* true.

MYTHELLANEOUS

Medicine

★ There is a cure for baldness
★ Nurses never laugh at a patient's condition
★ Doctors never discuss actual cases with their own families
★ Injections of lambs' thyroid glands keep you young
★ Anything can be stitched back on these days
★ All nurses are goers
★ All doctors have a faint smell of drink about them — medicinal purposes only
★ Doctors don't look after themselves
★ 'An apple a day . . .' is true
★ GPs have the worst handwriting in the world
★ They quite often miss when giving injections and accidentally jab the pillow or themselves

X-RATED

On-the-job jams

Birds do it, bees do it, even educated fleas do it, but if they did it like this, they'd lock 'em up and throw away the key. Here's an unhealthy abundance of vacuums, in-depth innuendo and folks who should be obscene and not heard. Public morals, private vices; there's little we enjoy seeing more than the righteous falling from grace. This chapter leaves no crevice unstuffed, and confirms the maxim that the higher the monkey climbs, the more he exposes. As for parental guidance, we advise you not to let your parents anywhere near this section — the chapter the censors couldn't understand. Not for the faint-hearted, the squeamish or the sexually adventurous (who wish to remain so) . . .

Kinky K.O.

A quiet Nottingham husband and wife, friendly with a work-mate of mine, were determined to spice-up their humdrum sex life. To this end, the bloke timidly visited a Private Shop in town, and came home with some pretty raunchy bondage gear.

They couldn't wait to try it out and within the hour they had it on. The wife was fastened to the bed in a star shape, while the husband elected, for some reason, to climb on top of a wardrobe, pretending to be a big cat moving in for the kill.

But at the crucial moment, he leapt down, hit his head on the bedframe, and knocked himself out cold for several hours. It fell to his unfortunate wife, still fastened in full tackle to the bed, to alert the neighbours so they could break in and set her free. The cul-de-sac was never as quiet again . . .

Lovers' lock

In the late seventies, two young people were making love in the back seat of a Mini (yes, it can be done), when due to a sudden muscular contraction and seizure, they were stuck fast. Luckily the woman was able to reach round her partner to press the horn and summon help. Soon after, the fire brigade were called, but try (and laugh) as they might, they couldn't liberate the lusty couple.

Eventually, there was no alternative but to cut the top off the car with oxy-acetylene gear and winch the still locked-together lovers out. The woman was in floods of tears, and a fireman tried to console her by explaining that there was nothing embarrassing about their predicament: 'We see things like this every day.'

'I know that,' said the woman, 'but what's my husband going to say when he sees the car . . .'

No small parts

Quite recently, according to a Nigerian friend, a film director in Lagos advertised in the local paper for male actors to star in a new porn film he was making.

The advert said that only amply proportioned men were sought, so 'those with less than eight inches to their credit need not apply'. Eventually, nearly three hundred well-hung hopefuls turned up for the audition.

Pinned on the door when they arrived was a sign explaining that the advert should have made clear the eight inches referred to girth, and not length. In the event, apparently only 24 of the 300 were rejected on grounds of size (!).

A sad reflection

Someone at work knows a quiet bloke who one day furtively asked someone else in the office if they had any hardcore porn videos he could borrow, as he'd got hold of two machines, and could copy them. He was lent one, and took it home to copy. But he wasn't too *au fait* with the workings of video recorders, and couldn't work out how to copy them direct.

Eventually, he resorted to what he knew: he set up his camcorder on a tripod and pointed it at the screen, recording the film as it played on his telly. When he returned the video to the lender, he explained the problems he'd had. So when he got home, the other bloke checked that the video he'd lent was all right. He was more than a little displeased at first to find out that the bloke had given him back the copy, not the original, but his annoyance soon turned to mirth.

The copy was a very poor recording, with a terrible glare from the TV screen, but as he looked closely, in the reflection he could make out the distinct image of his workmate kneeling in front of the box, gratifying himself.

Chicken gobble

A father was renowned for staying out late and falling asleep in front of the telly in a drunken stupor. It got to such a state that his teenage kids used to stick things on him when he was asleep.

One night, they got the neck from the giblets of a chicken they'd had for dinner, and placed it in their drunken father's fly, dangling down. In the morning, his wife nearly had a heart attack when she saw the cat licking and chewing what she mistook for something of a more intimate nature.

Give and give

A friend from Accrington went on holiday with his friends to Thailand, with a view to sampling the local hospitality.

On his first night, he went to a pick-up bar and enjoyed a few local cocktails. During the course of the evening he was approached by an absolutely beautiful prostitute, and after a few seconds' deliberation set his mind on bedding her.

A little later, he was being led back to a small, rough apartment round the corner from the bar. When they got down to it, the prostitute undressed teasingly, to reveal small pert breasts and . . . unmistakably male genitalia. Not a little taken aback, the bloke stammered, 'What am I supposed to do with that?!'

'You give me cock, I give you cock!' came the earnest reply.

Fit for nothing

Apparently, when someone suffers an epileptic fit, one of the main problems is that the victim's teeth clamp shut for the duration. That's why it's sadly quite common for epileptics to bite through their tongues.

Anyway, I heard about a couple who were out on Lovers' Lane one night in their car. Their motor was too small for anything but oral relief and they'd got up to a '68-er − 'You give me a blow-job and I'll owe you one' − with the woman seeing to her man first. Tragically, while *in flagrante delicto*, the woman suffered an epileptic fit and her jaws clamped horribly shut. In his pain the bloke tried to loosen her vice-like grip, unavoidably bruising her face rather badly. Eventually the fit passed and they drove painfully to hospital where they had to answer some awkward questions from smirking nurses about the injuries they'd sustained.

Tits first

When I was a DJ in Walkers Club, Newcastle, one of the regular clubbers told me a story about a Geordie lass he'd encountered.

He was dancing in the club and chatting up a real bonnie lass, who was coming on strong. He bought her a drink and they had a good laugh together. Shortly, she whispered that they should go back to her place, which they did.

So they were sitting on the sofa and the lad's hand started to wander up the Geordie girl's thigh. Suddenly she broke off, slapped his face and shouted indignantly:

'Where's yer manners, like? Tits first!'

The arty man's peculiar habit

A well-known New York musician has an odd habit, apparently. A woman acquaintance of a Manhattan friend of mine met him at a gallery opening night in trendy SoHo (which means south of Houston, apparently). She was excited and flattered that he showed a real interest in her.

They went back to his loft apartment and talked for hours, late into the night. Then, as if in a dream, they made love slowly and gently until they fell asleep.

In the morning, however, the woman awoke with a start and looked up to see this famous man crouching above her face, his buttocks primed for an affectionate loving . . .

Third leg thrombosis

My friend had a Spanish mate who was so randy he'd shag a barber's floor. He couldn't get enough. He'd often have three or four women on the go at a time and still not be satisfied.

However, he decided to settle down with the woman of his dreams and got married. For the first week of their marriage they were at it like a sewing machine. Even so, one night she awoke to find her husband masturbating in his sleep. Anyway, after ten days his libido got the better of his member and he waddled to a doctor in excruciating pain.

The doctor examined his part and exclaimed that he'd never come across anything like it: 'You've got thrombosis of the penis, *Señor.*'

These boots were made for wanking

One of the distractions of being in the fire service is the quirky lot that repeatedly call you out under false pretences. A friend in the Holloway service in London claims that one local crank often rings 999 knowing by law they have to check out his place no matter what. When they arrive, the door is open, they rush up a wooden staircase, and the bloke is there, suspended in the landing by leather and straps attached to his chest and wedding tackle, which he is fondling. Apparently, he gets off on the vibration of the firemen's heavy boots on the shaky staircase.

We still can't work out how he reaches the phone.

The photocopier philanderers

A couple kept an illicit relationship secret from the rest of their office in Leicester, for fear of the sack. Until, that is, one night, after everyone else had left for the day, they worked themselves up into a sexual frenzy. They thrashed around on the desks, the floor, and finally made love with abandon sitting on the photocopier. Imagine their red-faced surprise when the next morning they were confronted with dozens of facsimiles of their private parts festooned around the office . . .

Revenge is . . .

The husband of a woman my wife works with told me about a friend of his from home in Norwich who'd gone out to a disco with his mates. They'd all been drinking heavily to build up their courage, before seeking out the local talent in Cinderella's Nitespot. Before long they all tapped off — it was that kind of place — except this one bloke, who just kept on necking the ale all evening.

At the end of the night, he'd managed to strike lucky with a lass, who he took back to his place. They undressed and went to bed, even though he was really slaughtered and having trouble even raising a smile — let alone anything below the belt. After a few minutes foreplay, his head began to spin and, disappointingly, he threw up all over the woman and passed out flat on his back next to her. When he woke up, with a splitting headache, he was alarmed to see there was a small turd lying cleanly on his chest, but the woman who put it there was nowhere to be seen.

The next few should really be in the **Under the Knife** section, but were far too sordid . . .

Pipe down, sir

A friend whose boyfriend worked as a hospital porter in Rochdale hospital's casualty ward told me a number of stories about patients admitted with peculiar complaints.

One day he was working in the incinerator room at the back of the hospital, burning the old dressings and the like, when an ambulance pulled into the loading bay. The doors opened and a worried-looking man got out, wearing only a long mac, carrying a Hoover, and walking very gingerly. The sucking end of the vacuum pipe, obviously attached to something, emerged from his raincoat just below waist height.

The botty bottle

Another time, late at night, the porter was alerted to a commotion caused by a throng of nurses, some peeling away, hands over their mouths, to stifle the laughter, surrounding a terrified-looking bloke crouching face-down on a stretcher, and covered by a blanket.

It transpired that he had an old-style milk bottle firmly implanted up to the lip in his back passage. The victim explained that he'd been taking up some curtains in the kitchen when he'd slipped and sat on the bottle, which was upside down on the draining-board.

The force of his tumble had formed a vacuum and to remove the vessel, the surgeon only had two means at his disposal: either smash it, or find a means to get some purchase and pull it out. He decided on the second course, and carefully filled the bottle with plaster, slipping a stick inside before it set rock hard — a bit like making your own ice-lolly, really. Then, straining hard, he tugged it out with a pop.

Two weeks later, the same man was back with a similar problem — only this time, he'd 'fallen' on an old-style Coke bottle.

Rampant but broken

A sailor home on leave and his wife were in the middle of making love when she started coughing and asked her mate if he would mind nipping downstairs to fetch her a glass of water.

Not wanting her to 'go off the boil', he rushed down the stairs three at a time, hurtled into the kitchen, but unfortunately slipped on a discarded bar of soap and landed on his still-proud John Thomas, snapping him amidships.

Yes, it can happen . . .

Suds law

During the 1970s, when economic conditions led to the three-day working week, and we were all encouraged to 'Save It', one of the Tory government's suggestions was 'Save water, bath with a friend'. Two young newly-weds took this advice to heart with lusty enthusiasm, but dire consequences. Their bathtime foamy frolics created a vacuum in the coital area, and they were locked in soapy union. They managed to draw their neighbour's attention to the predicament, who naturally called in the fire brigade. The bath was cut free and the embarrassed couple were carried out past peering neighbours into a waiting ambulance.

Bangkok Bill

An Ashford, Kent, man went on business to Bangkok for a month, and took enthusiastic advantage of the local hospitality. Perhaps too enthusiastically — for after a week, he found his three-piece burning up with some strange infestation. Immediately he visited a clinic specialising in communicable diseases. He was diagnosed as having crab lice and had intensive, expensive treatment for the rest of his stay.

When he returned home, he decided not to come clean with his wife. But as luck would have it, one morning she was opening his mail over breakfast as usual and came across his American Express bill, which she always pored over with extra care.

This time, one particular entry caught her eye, and she called upstairs quizzically, 'Darling, what did you have done at the Bangkok Institute for Sexually Transmitted Diseases?'

> Sex and religion — an intoxicating mix, full of innocence, guilt and holy inappropriate behaviour . . .

Doggie-collar fashion

A speech therapist from a rural village near Sleaford, Lincolnshire, knew the local doctor very well, and on occasion, with the GP's customary disregard for patient confidentiality, he'd tell her about one of his juicy cases, leaving out the names, of course.

One evening he was particularly keen to relate the latest story. Apparently, a young vicar and his innocent wife in the village had come to him seeking advice about pregnancy. They'd stopped using contraceptives five years ago, and had been trying to conceive ever since without success.

Some time back, they'd also been to a clinic to establish their fertility, and the results showed that there was no medical reason for them not conceiving. As a last hope, the cleric and his dearly beloved had come to ask their doctor what they could do. He spent an hour talking things over with them, asking about ovulation days, cold baths and baggy Y-fronts, but all seemed fine.

Then, clutching at straws, the doctor asked them, 'How

exactly are you doing it?'

Reddening slightly, the vicar said, 'Just the same as everyone else, doctor. You know: put my tinkle against my wife's belly button, and jiggle up and down for twenty minutes.'

More cake, vicar?

A friend was a bit of a handful, in more ways than one — but more of that later. Anyway, he recently started a relationship with a lovely girl. Although they'd been going out for quite a while he had never been introduced to her parents and was very keen to meet the old fossils. He knew the father was a man of the cloth, but fancied getting a shufty at the old dear to see what his girlfriend would turn out like. The girlfriend seemed determined to prevent a get-together, probably with very good reason.

Then one day, out of the blue, she suggested going to her parents' house to sort through some of her old school things. He couldn't wait. However, when they arrived at the house he found, to his disappointment, that his girlfriend had arranged for her folks to be out. They went up to her bedroom and started sorting through the bric-a-brac. But one thing led to another and they ripped off their clothes, made mad, passionate love rolling around on the old exercise books, then dozed off.

A little later, he woke up on his own and, still naked, set out to find his girlfriend. When he got downstairs he could hear her in the front room listening to the radio. The door was slightly ajar so he decided to have a bit of fun. He propped up his abnormally large John Thomas between finger and thumb, waved it round the edge of the door, and squawked in a high-pitched Mr Punch voice, 'That's the way to do it! That's the way to do it!' There was no reaction, so he did it again. Still silence, so he popped his head round the door.

There, frozen amid the vicarage tea and cakes, was his girlfriend, red as a beetroot, and her astonished parents.

Sofa, so bad

A bloke at a friend's hockey club was a dirty old git, but those who live by the pork sword die by it. At the end of one game, he settled down like many of the others in the team to the 'mag' session, when the lads would get out their raunchy girlie magazines in the changing room and have a good ogle.

The dirty git was looking through the Reader's Wives section of one mucky book, and all of a sudden burst out laughing. 'Hey lads, look!' he shouted, pointing his finger at the pictures inside, 'my missus is in here this month!' Then he started, looked closer at the spread, turned a peculiar shade of puce, and muttered, 'But that's not my sofa . . .'

Below the belt

A friend's cousin was getting married, and his mates organised a drunken, seedy stag do above a pub in Stockwell, south London, for a dozen of his close mates. It was one of those stag nights you only seem to *hear* about, never get invited to. They'd organised some raunchy videos to start with, then at about 8.30 the 'girls' came on. Three local strippers did a live sex act on stage, and towards the end of their performance, they grabbed some of the lads (the ones wearing ties) and gave them the 'towel' treatment. Then they dragged them up on to the stage and made them do all sorts of filthy things with their clothes off. After the act had finished, some of the lads approached the girls about providing something a bit more private, and negotiations were carried out. Eventually, the drunken groom-to-be chatted one of them into giving him a blow-job for an extra £5. They adjourned to a side room, and he was given a quick seeing to. But his hand began to stray under the skirt of his partner, and to his horror his fingers encountered two hairy plums. The stripper was a man . . .

MYTHELLANEOUS

Sex

★ You can't get pregnant standing up
★ Women don't like it
★ Men do it more than women
★ Cats' have got hooks on the end
★ Welshmen prefer sheep
★ Dachshunds do it with Great Danes
★ Eighty-year-old men and women are always at it
★ Medical students cut off corpses' willies and sew them to the bottom of their trousers
★ Surely you know how they get the holes in doughnuts?
★ Pigs' ones are like corkscrews
★ It's protein innit!?
★ Catherine the Great preferred horses. As did Caligula
★ The Chinese are masters at penis transplants, and a man donated his member to his grandson because he no longer had any use for it

WEDDED BLISS

Nuptial nonsense

In common with many of life's ritual occasions, the rigmarole of matrimony has thrown up its own folk tales. The pressure to make it the perfect day is too much for most of us, and the potential banana skins rain down like confetti. The following twice-told stories show people at their most vulnerable being unceremoniously humiliated. Will you still want to catch the barbed bouquet after reading them?

The plastered groom

A friend of mine, a medical student, was out on his stag night. As you might expect, he got totally paralytic, and, for a prank, his friends dragged him back to their hospital and put both his legs in plaster from ankle to hip.

The next morning, the day of his wedding, he woke up still plastered (in both senses). He was in a right panic, but his best man explained that he was lucky: he'd had a really bad fall the night before and had been rushed to hospital.

So the groom had to hobble down the aisle on crutches, much to some people's amusement, and spent the whole reception still in plaster. His mates decided to tell him the truth when the couple arrived at their hotel on honeymoon.

Everyone cheered them off as they drove away, and thinking enough was enough, someone rang the hotel and left a message that his legs were okay really, and he could remove the plaster.

Unfortunately, to prevent any tricks being played on the newly-weds while at their nuptials, the groom had deliberately given his friends the name of the wrong hotel.

Mr and Mrs

A friend of mine was at a wedding reception that was a real laugh. The stag night was mad enough, but at the reception after the ceremony they did a 'Mr and Mrs'-type question and answer quiz with the bride and groom, asking each in turn intimate questions about the other, who had his or her ears covered while this was going on.

First to go was the groom, a right cocky so-and-so. They asked him various things about his new wife, and then:

'Where's the most unusual place you've had sex?' That really got people going.

'Easy,' said the groom, 'on the kitchen sink.' There were howls of embarrassed laughter. So they brought the bride back, a shy girl who didn't like this at all. Everything went okay until the same question.

'Where's the most embarrassing place you've had sex?'

The bride went as white as her dress and looked over to her husband distraught, whispering 'I can't, I can't.' He was laughing his head off and said, 'Don't worry, love, I've already said. It's okay.'

Still not sure, the bride turned round and answered: 'Up the bottom.'

> That one really has been doing the rounds recently, and we've been told at least five different versions. All those who told it swore they were there, of course, but does Derek Batey, former compère of the old afternoon quiz show itself, know what a huge cult he's made of himself?

Hostile reception

Some close friends recently went to a remarkable wedding in Liverpool of some people they didn't know very well. The marriage spanned a strong religious divide: the bride's family were firm Irish Catholics and the groom's lot devout Protestants.

Lots of the bride's relatives had come over from the Emerald Isle on the ferry, all big lads who'd been drinking since breakfast. But the day seemed to pass off okay, despite some tension. Everyone was on their best behaviour for the couple, though the groom seemed a bit wooden despite the attentions of his lovely bride. Everyone put it down to nerves.

The best man's speech was quite a hit, but the groom didn't laugh once. When it was his turn to speak, the groom shuffled to his feet, thanked the in-laws, the caterers and all the usual stuff.

Then, turning to his bride, he said 'Finally, I'd like to thank my best man Kevin for sleeping with my new wife Bernadette for the last six months, I hope you'll both be very happy together,' and he walked out of the hall without looking back.

The place erupted and the whole reception ended in disaster, with Protestant against Catholic in a huge unholy brawl that spilled out into the road and was only stopped when some of the blood-stained guests were arrested by the police.

> Needless to say, the couple didn't even go on their honeymoon . . . This secular Scouse scenario was recently adapted by Harry Enfield for his TV show, with the same denouement.

Ultra-violet embarrassment

A workmate's brother was getting hitched and went out on

a stag night bender with all his mates from the football club.

They were living it up until the early hours, and when he woke up the next day the groom had a stinking hangover and looked deathly pale. So on the way to the church the best man took him to a solarium, with the idea that he'd look better in the wedding photographs.

They had quite some time to spare so the groom settled himself on the sun bed and closed his eyes. Two hours later he woke up with a start, ripped off his goggles, put on his clothes and dashed to the church.

Everyone was sniggering as he took his place, and his wife was horrified when she saw how he looked: his face was sunburnt scarlet apart from around his eyes, where the goggles had left big white patches. He looked like a panda. Which was handy because they were off to China for their honeymoon.

Up and under

A friend was getting married and against all advice chose as his best man the biggest scoundrel in the rugby club. The bloke selected was a lewd, raucous oaf who rarely overlooked the chance to stick one on someone (in or out of the scrum) or show someone up, and he was always bragging about how many ten-pence pieces he could carry in his foreskin — £1.80 at the last attempt. (Others in the club said this meant he was 'all skin and no sausage', but that's by-the-by.)

Everyone — especially the anxious bride-to-be — was horrified at what the consequences of the groom's decision might be. But, completely out of character, the best man behaved perfectly. He kept the groom sober on his stag night, handled the wedding arrangements professionally, was extremely polite to all the relatives, and, amazingly, made an inoffensive speech.

Even the bride gave him a peck on the cheek in thanks, as the reformed best man waved the glowing couple off on their honeymoon at the end of a perfect day.

The newly-weds spent a wonderfully passionate nuptial night in a quaint country cottage hotel, making full use of all the intimate honeymoon suite's facilities.

The morning after, they woke late and kissed tenderly. The groom picked up the phone, rang up room service and asked for two cups of tea to be brought up.

'Make that three,' bellowed the best man's voice from under the bed.

> Okay, so the bit about the coins was a slight embellishment, but we knew a rugger-bugger who performed similar tricks and claimed the same record . . . but then he was from Pontefract.

Blue wedding video

Some friends went to a top-drawer wedding in Bath, where everything was planned to perfection: the white Rolls, 5k wedding dress, top hat, tails, the lot.

The bride's parents had spent a fortune and understandably wanted the big day captured for posterity on video. They'd hired what they thought was a top-notch local outfit to do the job.

On the day, the weather was great, not a cloud in the sky and everyone looked fabulous, especially the radiant bride. A wonderful time was had by all, and everyone was looking forward to seeing the video after it had been edited.

It just so happened that the bride's folks were down the weekend the finished product arrived. The newly-weds excitedly ripped open the package, made a pot of tea and they all sat down to watch the lovely film.

But there must have been a mix-up at the video company, and they were shocked at what they saw on the film: there in vivid colour was the slimy video cameraman and some sweaty overnight male friends romping naked in a series of compromising scenarios.

> [*If this story is right up your alley, check out the* **X-rated** *section*]

MYTHELLANEOUS

Weddings

★ At joint weddings, you can end up with the wrong bride if you're not careful

★ If the wedding's not consummated it doesn't count

★ At the reception, a drunken uncle always has to say to one of the bride's friends, 'If only I was ten years younger . . .'

★ The best man always gets the bridesmaid

★ Everyone loves a wedding

★ Bridesmaids look lovely in pink nylon, puff-sleeve, princess-line dresses

★ Elderly relatives always button their jackets up wrongly for the photos

★ Brides' mothers and grooms' mothers always wear the same hat

★ Everyone loves the 'Birdie Song'

FRIENDS AND RELATIONS

With friends like these, who needs relatives?

The 'there but for the grace of god . . .' section. Family feuds and errant kids in one corner, vengeful mates and humiliating first dates in the other, all laced together with a warped sense of class solidarity. These apocryphal tales resassure you that if you think you're having a bad day, there's always someone in the same boat as you, but with a bad case of biliousness, lost false teeth and a spouse that's out to do damage, thrown in for good measure. Remember, there's only a 'why?' between blood relatives and 'bloody relatives!' . . .

Atlantic potion

As is quite common among British families, my pal's parents in Essex had an elderly aunt and uncle in Canada who had emigrated decades earlier. The *émigrés* retained a nostalgia for home, but at the same time felt they had bettered themselves and tried to help out their kin who stayed behind by regularly sending them examples of the good life they enjoyed in the new world, like food or electrical gadgets.

One year, nothing arrived for a long, long time. The family began to wonder how their Canadian folks were, but correspondence remained unanswered.

Then after several months a package arrived from Canada. It was a Jiffy bag containing a little box with what looked like powered soup inside. How typically sweet of them! But there was no note with the soup, so the family drank it still unaware of how their aunt and uncle were.

Two days later, an air mail letter arrived from Canada. It was from their aunt, apologising for not keeping in touch, but explaining that she had spent all her time nursing her husband for the last six months before he died.

On his death-bed he had made her promise that he would be buried on English soil. 'But I couldn't send his body back, and so I had him cremated. I sent his ashes in a separate parcel, and I know you'll see to it that your uncle is given a suitable send-off,' concluded the letter.

[*See also* Odd customs, **Travel Sickness**]

Just after the Second World War, it was

commonplace for relatives who'd been evacuated or emigrated to Canada or Australia to send food parcels back to rationing-hit Britain. The sort of thing in the last story happened all the time. Nowadays, the ex-pat relatives are renowned for thinking younger members of the family they left behind are stuck in some kind of pre-pubescent time warp, and sending thirty-somethings cowboy suits and *Cat In The Hat* books for their birthdays. That's Canada for you.

A fart amongst friends

A Fulham lass my wife's sister knows is always getting herself into scrapes, usually over new boyfriends. This occasion was no exception. She had just met a really dishy posh bloke, who had invited her to a party with his friends. Determined to impress him, she dolled herself up in a tight, classy little black number.

At the party, though, she was so nervous that a certain amount of biliousness welled up inside her and threatened to make itself heard in the form of a loud trumpet, so that she couldn't relax at all. What made it worse was that every time she tried to give vent to her flatulence in private, her guy sought her out with a smile and sidled up next to her. The queue to the lav stretched down the stairs, so no point in waiting for that either.

Eventually, her boyfriend came over to her and said, to her relief, that they were going now. Holding in the noxious wind for just a little longer while the bloke escorted her to his car and let her in, she was even more relieved when he finally left her side, saying he'd forgotten to get someone's telephone number.

With immense satisfaction, she sat in the passenger seat and let fly the most enormous rasping fart.

A minute later, her man opened the driver's side to get in. 'Sorry, I've been terribly rude – have you met Carol and Peter,' he said, pointing to two embarrassed friends silently holding their noses in the back of the car.

> With tasteful adjustments, that scenario was used in the TV sit-com *Just Good Friends*. But this next one was obviously beyond salvation; Jan Francis' danger money would've been too high . . .

That sinking feeling

The same young lady, apparently, was involved in an equally excruciating episode with another posh bloke. On this occasion, she was invited to the young man's swanky Knightsbridge town-house to meet his parents. She'd never been to a really big, upmarket mansion, and she was on her best behaviour.

It was a very formal meal, and everything was just so until she needed to use the toilet. Worried that asking for the 'lav' was crass and common, she tried to recall the posh way to say it. Then she remembered, and asked her boyfriend's mother 'for the cloakroom'.

The mother gave her directions to an upstairs room, but when the young woman opened the door, it was exactly that: a cloakroom with coats, etc., but no toilet, just a small wash-basin.

By now desperate for a leak, the lass hitched up her taffeta dress and jumped up to sit over the sink to relieve herself. Halfway through, however, there was a nasty crack and the sink came away from the wall. The huge crash was heard downstairs and the diners rushed up to check on their guest.

When they opened the door, they found her sprawled over the smashed porcelain with two painfully twisted ankles, and her knickers round her knees, in a suspicious-looking puddle.

> Both these stories epitomise the powerful element of class conflict in apocryphal stories, and the idea that you should 'stick to your own' and not get above your station. Social climbing, it seems, always ends in a fall. [*See also* The chamber pot, **Urban Classics**]

Going down

An elderly couple lived in a ramshackle old terraced house, one of the first in its street to have an inside toilet. Now the old codger was a bit of a drinker and was none too fussy about his toilet habits, or shall we say accuracy. He always missed the target and nearly always left the seat up, much to his wife's annoyance.

This went on for years and years, until one day the old dear, who was rather big-boned, went upstairs to use the convenience. Finding the seat aloft again, she slammed it in place and sat down, rather more heavily than usual.

The rotted floorboards gave way and she crash-landed on the kitchen table in front of her startled husband, still astride the privvy.

> More bog-standard humour required? *See* Flushed with embarrassment, **Under the Knife**.

The yuppies' saucy neighbours

An 'upwardly mobile' young couple moved to a new cul-de-sac just outside Hertford, and were surprised to be asked to one of those 'partner-swapping' sessions almost as soon as they settled in.

For a laugh, they agreed to take part, and on the evening in question threw the keys to their car — a brand new white BMW — into the hat along with all the others on the close. Then each woman picked out a pair of keys and went off with the man who owned them.

The yuppie wife picked out hers and (much to her husband's grief) seemed very excited at her hunky selection, who she ran off with.

There were about a dozen couples in total, but when all the car keys had been picked out, the yuppie bloke still hadn't been approached. When he was left all alone in the room, he sulkily trudged home, noting with bitterness that his treasured BMW was no longer parked outside.

The odd thing was, his wife returned, but his car never

did. Naturally, he didn't dare try to tell his story to the police.

The Xmas family break-in

A nice family from Berwick, three sons in their twenties and a retired couple, planned to spend the Christmas holiday with in-laws at their new semi in Winchmore Hill, north London. They were due to arrive late on Xmas Eve, so the in-laws agreed to leave the side gate open and a back door key under a stone in the garden for them.

The family arrived even later than they thought, because the map the in-laws had sent them was useless. Exhausted, they finally came across the tree-lined road, followed the numbers and parked outside. One of the sons went to open the side gate, but it was locked, so he scrambled over the top. Then he unlocked the gate for the others, and they all stumbled about in the garden trying to find the stone and the key.

Then one of them hissed that the back door was open anyway, so they strolled in and collapsed in the lounge before unloading their stuff and making a pot of tea and sandwiches as quietly as possible. The mother, nosing around at her brother's new house, noticed some framed photos on the TV, but wasn't that surprised when she didn't recognise the people shown, even an old wedding shot of a couple she'd never seen before.

After their refreshments, the tired travellers crept upstairs, found empty rooms and went to bed. The next morning, Xmas Day, they all trooped downstairs for breakfast, and were confronted by two complete strangers sitting at the table. They had accidentally broken into the house next door.

The spurned wife

A friend swears this happened to one of his mates at work.
This fellow was walking home down a swanky avenue one
sunny evening, and passed a big house with a Porsche in
the drive. On the car's windscreen there was a hand-written
sign saying '£5 – everything must go!'

Intrigued, he knocked on the front door. Presently, a
tearful, bedraggled woman answered. He asked her about
the car, and she distractedly said yes, it *was* only a fiver.
Seriously? Yes seriously.

Absolutely made up, he handed over a Harold Melvin (blue
note, savvy?), and she gave him the keys and log book. Then
she asked him if he needed any golf clubs, or hi-fi, or
designer suits, or an exercise bike, dirt cheap. Now getting
a little suspicious, the fellow asked what all this was about.

The woman replied with tears in her eyes that her cheating
husband had told her he was going away on business, but
she had found out he was really having it away with his
secretary in Venice.

So she'd arranged quite a big surprise for him when he
returned home, and was selling off everything he owned for
sod all.

> One of the perennial fantasies of the hard-up
> motorist, that one, and part of the broader
> urban mythology theme of 'something for

nothing'. Another car scam is the once widely held belief that if the numbers in the price stuck on the window of a showroom car happen to fall off, the new price stands. It's created a rash of supposedly true stories about people spotting that a few zeros have blown off the screen of a Rolls-Royce and snapping up the glamour motor, after some argument, for a paltry sum, because it's the law.

Down the hatch

This actually happened to a friend of mine from Camden. He was round at his girlfriend's parents' house for the first time, and they were having a very polite meal together.

Nerves (and a beans-on-toast luncheon) were playing havoc with him and he had an untimely case of bad wind. Excusing himself, he swiftly left the table and rushed to the toilet, but on the way spotted a little open window and simply thrust his bottom through the hole and guffed loudly.

Shortly, he returned to the silent dinner table. The rest of the evening passed without mishap, for which my mate was very grateful.

In the car on the way home, the lad turned to his quiet girlfriend and said, 'Well, I thought it went very well. What do'you reckon, darling?'

'I reckon it was going fine until you farted through the serving hatch . . . darling.'

The old man and the teeth

My uncle's a bit of a fisherman and he knows a bunch of ancient anglers — all of them must be over seventy if they're a day — who like to go off on fishing weekends to get away from their wives (which is a relief for their wives too). One time they decided to try their luck at sea-fishing off Grimsby and set off early, in a convoy of old bangers.

Unfortunately, the briny started to cut up rough into a heavy swell as soon as the crusty old codgers were afloat. The boat was pitching and rolling and they all felt pretty green. One particularly queasy old gimmer lost his breakfast over the side, and with it his false teeth, to his great annoyance and the huge amusement of the others.

Later, when the sea was much calmer, another old bloke hooked a large mackerel. For a joke, he slit open the fish, took out his own false choppers and slipping them inside, called to the bloke who'd chucked up, 'Would you believe it? Look: this here fish has swallowed your teeth!'

'Give it here,' said the choppery old fogey, snatching the set of teeth, and slipping them on to his gums. Then he grinned, spat them into his hand and chucked them over the side, saying, 'Naw, they're not mine.'

Kids don't appear too often as victims in apocryphal tales — that would be *too* sick — and are not even that common as main characters. But they do love to tell them. Many of the stories we came across in researching this book struck a chord that had last resonated in the playground or in pubescent conversation — especially the vindictive 'Lovers' Lane' tales and others in the **Urban Classics** section. If anything, though, this next little collection shows the sweeter, cheekier side of childsplay, not the Terminator within. [*See* **Technophobia** *for the sordid side*]

The hyperactive zoo child

It was Easter bank holiday and some friends of the family were off to Dudley Zoo for a treat. Their little lad was the hyperactive type, allergic to chocolate or something. He just couldn't sit still, always up to some mischief or other, and generally getting into hair-raising scrapes. His mother had decided that as zoos can be very dangerous places, she'd keep a firm hold of his hand, but after ten minutes of him fidgeting, wriggling and moaning she was glad to be shot of him and he scampered away.

He was running riot, fooling around inside the safety rail of the lions' cage, climbing into the monkey enclosure, leaning right over the parapet of the polar bears' pool and even balancing on the edge of the crocodile pit throwing bread. His folks just couldn't keep up with him. When it was time to go, the parents spent twenty minutes calling him. Eventually, he slunk towards them with his arms crossed, and got into the car. On the way home he was strangely quiet and ran straight upstairs when they got back. His jaded parents sloped into the kitchen for a well-earned cup of tea, but were disturbed by a rumpus coming from upstairs.

Imagine their surprise when they opened the bathroom door

to see their little treasure splashing about in the bath with a small, bewildered penguin.

The coveted pom-pom hat

Two young sisters really hated each other. For some reason, the elder sister coveted a new pom-pom hat owned by the younger one, and one evening nicked it off her head, putting it on herself and skipping down the street.

As if by fate, at that moment, a bat swooped down and flew off with the hat.

Par for pa

My father's friend was involved in an amusing episode brought about by the unstinting affection of his eight-year-old son.

Every now and then, he used to organise a round of golf with his boss — say when he wanted to ask for a pay rise or bigger company car — and, much against his fiercely competitive nature, would deliberately lose, even though his boss was a hopeless player. He knew that if he beat the old man on the links, the chances of ameliorating his work conditions were as slim as a lady's putter.

Nevertheless, after one of these rounds, the fellow would return home in a stinking mood, having had to hit balls into the water and the rough, and bite his lip when the boss got too patronising. His young son saw the effect these occasions had on his dad, and hatched a plan to cheer him up.

The next time they were due to play happened to fall during the school summer holiday. They set off for a nearby course, unaware that the avenging son was making his own way down there.

At the first tee, the bloke hit a reasonable drive. His boss sliced his ball behind some trees as usual. When he found it, the ball was all but buried in mud. If he didn't know better, the boss would've thought someone had stamped on it.

He hacked the ball just a few yards. His partner gritted his teeth — this meant he'd have to play even worse now. But the first hole set the pattern for the rest of the round. Every time the boss's ball went out of sight, it either disappeared completely, ended up deep in the ground, or seemed to have travelled an extra thirty yards into some water.

And every time, the other fellow was forced to lower his game to compensate. Both men grew more and more angry until the 18th, when the boss topped his drive just over the hill, and straining to see where it went, caught sight of a little lad in a red shell suit, who ran over to his ball and stamped on it again and again.

His partner saw the boy, too, and was shamed to recognise him as his own son, but kept quiet about that detail. But the boss turned to him with the look of a mad bull:

'That's your bloody son, isn't it! Well he and his mischief have just cost you the promotion I was going to offer you.' The bloke returned home, threw down his clubs and lunged at his son . . . before bursting out laughing and thanking him for making sure he never had to go through that humiliating golf ritual again.

This little piggy extra

A friend of my sister's and her husband were playing with their eighteen-month-old toddler and getting her ready for a bath. To settle her down while the water was running, they started playing 'Piggy' with her foot:

'This little piggy went to market,
This little piggy went to town,
This little piggy had roast beef,
And this little piggy had none,
And this little piggy went wee wee wee all the way home.'
But oddly there was still one toe on her foot left to tweak.

> Now here's an oddity: scientists have discovered that the gene that produces six toes is actually dominant. It's even said that in one particular area of Utah, America, if you're not six-toed and a dwarf, you're considered strange – a local factory even makes wider shoes to cater for this market. Apparently, six-toed people are over-represented in sports where balance is an asset – unlike the following game, where being an incurable insomniac can have its advantages.

Sunday best, personal best

A Northampton businessman in his fifties was excitedly anticipating the start of the cricket season. Even though he wasn't very good at the game, being British it wasn't the winning but the taking part he loved, especially the social life. So much so that his wife was a cricket widow.

Seeing her husband so happy and the chance of any DIY being done for the next three months diminishing made the wife see red, and she took the drastic action of burning all his cricket gear, just before the first match of the season.

Undaunted, he turned out for his village team in his Sunday best grey suit — and curiously scored a half century, his finest ever knock.

Go ferret

A Barnsley lad kept ferrets and enjoyed nothing better than to carry one round in his trousers. Contrary to popular belief, the creatures don't bite or wriggle. The motion usually just makes them lie still, giving a warm glow to your nether regions.

Anyhow, this lad was one day courting a lass, and opted for taking her to the pictures. It was only when he picked her up on the way that he remembered he still had one of the ferrets down his kecks.

He was aware that the lass might be quite shocked by the grubby rodent, so he resolved to keep it in his baggies for the duration. However, towards the end of the film, as they tucked into the last of their snacks, the lass felt someone having a good go at her popcorn.

'Bloody cheek,' she thought, annoyed at her boyfriend, 'he's just polished off a packet himself.'

But the attack on her popcorn continued, and she slapped her hand down to stop him – and screamed alarmingly. Just then the house lights went up, and the lass screamed again.

There was the ferret, stretching out of the lad's flies, still tucking into her sweets.

> Why do people put ferrets down their trousers?
> It's got to be risky, but probably a lot less risky
> than a mongoose in your boxer shorts. (Think
> about it . . .)

Brick house

According to a mate, when his uncle first came over from India during the sixties to live in Derby, he was unable to read or write English.

To make matters worse, on the street where he lived, all the front doors were painted the same colour green. So in the early days, to remind himself of where he lived the chap left a brick by the front gate.

But one evening during the first week he walked down his road to see all the local kids playing hopscotch with stones.

His marker was nowhere to be seen. It took him three hours and several embarrassing approaches to the wrong house before he found his own home again.

The next day, he left home with a pot of paint and left a bright white flash permanently on the pavement.

Ewe must be joking

A popular young person's myth, this one, and

though we've heard several versions of it,
we've yet to meet anyone who can say, when
pressed, that they witnessed it first hand.

Twin girls, who loved to play jokes on other inmates at their
boarding school in Berkshire, became the subject of a plot
by those they'd caught out during the year.

Come one weekend recess, the twins got their
comeuppance – big time. The other girls in their year
contrived to empty the twins' room of all their belongings
– every single last thing including the beds – and rolled
some turf they'd got hold of over the floor.

The finishing touch ended the episode with a flourish: two
sheep were rustled and locked in the twins' room to graze.

Fall guy

A similar and equally widespread student story is always set
in somewhere like Imperial College, where the student halls
are in high-rise blocks. The reason for this will become clear.

A lad, who's a bit of a tosser and fancies himself as a tough
guy, goes out celebrating his twenty-first birthday in a big
way. But while he's out, some of his fellow students plot
his downfall. They take all his personal possessions, including his clothes, bedspread, nicknacks and girlie pin-ups from
his room on the sixteenth floor, and relocate them in a
ground-floor apartment in the same block, setting his new
room up exactly as the old one was.

Meantime, the boor is getting roaring drunk and aggressive

as usual — more so as his drinks have been spiked all evening. When the bar closes, he's carried home by some mates, who are clued up about the scam. So when they get him in the lift, they make sure he can't see what buttons they press and go up a few floors, then back down to the ground, where they carry him out and into his room. When they get him in there, some of the lads start on him, goading him until he offers someone out. Then some of them grab and blindfold him, open the window, and start to throw him out. The others make like they're panicking, saying, 'Stop, you'll kill him!' and stuff. The bloke meanwhile is being held out of the window and still thinks he's on the sixteenth floor, so that he's absolutely bricking it. When they eventually let go of him, he falls four feet — and ruins a decent pair of Y-fronts. . .

MYTHELLANEOUS

Folk

★ The only reason we humans can speak is because we've got thumbs

★ Everyone's got a third eye, but hardly anyone knows how to use it

★ When a limb gets hacked off, you don't feel it, because you're in shock

★ You know what they say about blokes: big nose, big . . .

★ You know what they say about women: small mouth, small . . .

★ Small people have got a chip on their shoulder — look at Napoleon

★ Fat people float better

★ Thin people can't swim very well

★ You're actually taller first thing in the morning, and you weigh less when you're asleep

★ In a thousand years time, humans will have evolved into eight-foot-tall, one-fingered, bald monopods with a brain the size of a basketball

WANTED

If you have any Urban Myths you'd like to pass on, we would dearly love to hear about them. (If, on the other hand, you believe that any of the events depicted in *Urban Myths* actually happened to *you*, we know a very good medical student . . .)

Kindly send your stories to:

Phil Healey and Rick Glanvill, Planet X, 97 St John's Street, London EC1M 4AS

BIBLIOGRAPHY

DALE, Rodney *It's true ... It happened to a friend* (Duckworth, 1984)
BRUNVAND, Jan Harold *The Choking Doberman and other 'new' urban legends* (Norton, 1986)